The WAC Journal

Writing Across the Curriculum
Volume 23
November 2012

EDITOR
Roy Andrews

EDITORIAL BOARD
Art Young, Clemson University
Neal Lerner, Northeastern University
Carol Rutz, Carleton College
Meg Petersen, Plymouth State University
Terry Zawacki, George Mason University

REVIEW BOARD
Jacob S. Blumner, University of Michigan, Flint
Patricia Donahue, Lafayette College
John Eliason, Gonzaga University
Michael LeMahieu, Clemson University
Neal Lerner, Northeastern University
Meg Petersen, Plymouth State University
Mya Poe, Pennsylvania State University
Carol Rutz, Carleton College
Joanna Wolfe, University of Louisville
Terry Zawacki, George Mason University
David Zehr, Plymouth State University

MANAGING EDITOR
Jared Jameson

ASSOCIATE EDITORS
David Blakesley
Michael LeMahieu

SUBSCRIPTIONS
Angie Justice
The WAC Journal
601 Strode Tower
Clemson University
Clemson, SC 29634
ajstc@clemson.edu | (864) 656-1520

SUBMISSIONS: The editorial board of The WAC Journal seeks WAC-related articles from across the country. Our national review board welcomes inquiries, proposals, and ten- to fifteen-page double-spaced manuscripts on WAC-related topics, including the following: WAC Techniques and Applications; WAC Program Strategies; WAC and WID; WAC and Writing Centers; Interviews and Reviews. Proposals and articles outside these categories will also be considered. MLA or APA citation style is acceptable. Send inquiries, proposals, or manuscripts to Roy Andrews via email (wacjournal@parlorpress.com).

The WAC Journal is peer-reviewed . It is published annually by Clemson University, Parlor Press, and the WAC Clearinghouse.

SUBSCRIPTIONS: *The WAC Journal* publishes one volume annually in print and is also available at The WAC Clearinghouse in digital format for free download. Print subscriptions support the ongoing publication of the journal and make it possible to offer digital copies as open access: One year: $25 | Three years: $65 | Five years: $95 | Please make your check payable to *Clemson University*. Include your email address and mailing address. Beginning January, 2013, a credit card payment option will be available online. Reproduction of material from this publication, with acknowledgement of the source, is hereby authorized for educational use in non-profit organizations.

© 2012 Clemson University
Printed on acid-free paper in the United States of America
ISSN 1544-4929

Contents

The WAC Journal
Volume 23, November 2012

ARTICLES

Changing Research Practices and Access: The Research Exchange Index   7
JENN FISHMAN & JOAN MULLIN

Crossing the Measurement and Writing Assessment Divide:
The Practical Implications of Inter-Rater Reliability in Faculty Development   19
JENNIFER GOOD

Articulating Claims and Presenting Evidence: A Study of Twelve
Student Writers, From First-Year Composition to
Writing Across the Curriculum   31
J. PAUL JOHNSON & ETHAN KRASE

From High School to College: Developing Writing Skills in the Disciplines   49
VIRGINIA CRANK

Spectators at Their Own Future: Creative Writing Assignments in the
Disciplines and the Fostering of Critical Thinking   65
ALEXANDRIA PEARY

INTERVIEW
Joe Harris: Teaching Writing Via the Liberal Arts   83
CAROL RUTZ

REVIEW   93
Writing in Knowledge Societies, edited by Doreen Starke-Meyerring,
Anthony Paré, Natasha Artemeva, Miriam Horne, and Larissa Yousoubova
Reviewed by MYA POE

Contributors   99
Subscribing to *The WAC Journal*   103

Changing Research Practices and Access: The Research Exchange Index

JENN FISHMAN & JOAN MULLIN

AT THE START OF THE RECENT International Writing Across the Curriculum (WAC) Research Workshop we conducted with Mike Palmquist, participants brainstormed research ideas. Across small groups of diverse colleagues from two- and four-year institutions, a single, driving question emerged: "What kind of research do I really need?" For some workshop participants, the question arose in relation to the perennial challenges presented by colleagues who want answers to these questions: Why should I, as an expert in my own field, have to teach writing? How can you, as an expert in writing, help my department and me? And, really, why can't students learn what they need in first-year writing? For others, this question was yoked to pedagogy: What are students really getting out of the writing intensive courses offered at my institution? How can I judge the effectiveness of a new assignment? Should I try portfolio grading? And yet another group, which was perhaps the largest, was motivated by overarching programmatic concerns: What kind of research will convince others that writing is central to learning? What should be the relationship between first-year writing and WAC courses? What can I learn by comparing outcomes with similar schools in my region, across the country, and around the world?

Our workshop group was aware of available resources from WAC Clearinghouse publications to CompPile, as well as recent traditionally published research useful for supporting WAC. In addition to these easily accessible texts, inquiries in genre studies and cultural-historical activity theory, the more recent ethnographic and quantitative studies summarized in *Researching the Writing Center: Towards an Evidence-Based Practice* (Babcock and Thonus), and work on transfer (e.g., Downs and Wardle, Nowacek) speaks to the burgeoning interest in WAC research. This current work answers the call posed by John Ackerman in "The Promise of Writing to Learn," underscored by Martha Townsend in "WAC Program Vulnerability and

What to Do About It: An Update and Brief Bibliographic Essay," and issued by Richard Haswell in "NCTE/CCCC's Recent War on Scholarship" (62-63). However, published, research-based scholarship, bibliographies, and online journal sites require that WAC scholars be current with past research and keep up with all the new materials, that they already know what research questions would best serve a particular program, and that they have access to abstracts or actual journal articles for theories and models of scholarship that best suit their specific context. Perhaps most important, our workshop participants wanted more detailed information about recent and ongoing work that could inform their next steps in conducting relevant, doable, applicable research.

These needs are no less important now than they were in 1988. It was then that Toby Fulwiler outlined what makes WAC programs successful; now, with more than thirty years of WAC history behind us, Townsend recognizes how relevant Fulwiler's statements remain, not least because the obstacles to program success he enumerates are still largely true across populations. Fulwiler noted problems with ongoing confusion about program nomenclature (62), poorly paced program growth rates (62-63), nonstandard administrative structures (63), and amorphous, open-ended program structures (63-64). Townsend neatly summarizes what remain as three obstacles related to research and program success: "WAC programs are result oriented, not research oriented" (47), "measures [of students' writing and learning development] that are quick and dirty do not seem to prove much" (47-48), and "evaluating successful WAC programs is as complicated as evaluating good teaching or successful learning" (48).

Given the complicated, interconnected nature of WAC, knowledge about and quick access to research in programmatic, curricular, and pedagogical areas is crucial. The newly developed Research Exchange Index (REx; http://researchexchange.colostate.edu/) will provide such knowledge and access in the form of a searchable database that contains short reports detailing the nitty-gritty of what researchers do, with whom, and why they do it: What were researchers' initial questions? What research did they draw on to plan their studies? What methods did they use on what population(s)? What were their earliest findings? What would they have changed in their study, and what are their questions now? While many of these details are woven into published scholarship, REx contains concise records of research activity, which make it possible to conduct swift and focused searches across each other's questions, methods, and reflections. Based on search results, REx readers can survey research activity in a particular area, find models for their own projects, or invite a colleague to collaborate on a new project. Equally important, REx includes information about research not readily available: ad hoc, local studies that are not published, that may be, at most, buried in a conference presentation or briefly referenced on a listserv.

Quite often such unavailable resources fall into the RAD and RFM categories. Although RAD (replicable, aggregable, and data-driven research) is the more familiar and at times more controversial term, RFM research is equally as important. Defined by Richard Haswell in "Documenting Improvement," replicable, feasible, and meaningful research (RFM) is key to contemporary researchers, whether they are teachers trying to design projects that will be "doable" during busy semesters or program administrators hoping to gather more than just numbers to share with colleagues. While the tendency has been to elide RAD and RFM research with published research, REx brings these different types of research together, setting records of published work alongside records of rigorously planned and carried out, *unpublished* RAD and RFM projects. Believing that published and unpublished academic work, qualitative and quantitative, RAD and RFM, all go hand in hand, REx emphasizes the relational aspects of the variety of our research by making visible information about how researchers construct knowledge through their work with each other, their subjects, and their audiences.

Inverse Proportions: More Research, Less Access

Multiple factors have led to a resurgence of research in WAC over the last twenty years. Across campuses, the growth of writing curricula has been matched by the growth of degree-granting programs and tracks at all levels, BA to PhD. Old and new programs alike have been subject to both internal and external pressure to meet and exceed benchmarks designed to measure efficacy and success, while tenure-line faculty (in particular) have faced increased pressure to publish, whether in traditional formats (i.e., articles, scholarly monographs) or in emerging forms of publication. These contradictory forces of expansion and narrowing support traditional humanities scholarship at the same time they create the need for new forums of scholarly exchange. Such demands have expanded listservs, conferences, and publications in all areas of writing studies (e.g., *Administrative Theory and Practice, Argumentation and Advocacy, Bulletin for the Association of Business Communication, Cross-Cultural Communication, Diálogos Latinoamericanos, Journal of Writing in Creative Practice*). While these platforms enhance our access to new work and ideas, they also make it impossible to keep up—to chart the development of a methodology, map the trajectory of a specific subfield, or review available research to situate a new study.

Theresa Lillis and Mary Jane Curry's multiyear study of academic writing and publishing by multilingual scholars seeking publication in English medium journals raises additional concerns for all writing researchers: gatekeeping. As Lillis and Curry demonstrate, "The politics of text production and evaluation and specific ideologies—including those about language, location and reviewing practices—are often rendered invisible" (161). For the most part, both old and new scholarly forms are produced by researchers in specific, often privileged professional situations where they are obligated to but also rewarded for producing certain kinds of scholarly texts. Also invisible much of the time are the ways in which these researchers rely on each other to build journals and participate in publications. This professional collaboration results in excellent scholarship, but as Lillis and Curry found, that work can exclude a broad sweep of research and researchers. For multilingual scholars, "[T]he centripetal pull towards the dominant practices and ideologies in the Anglophone centre ensures that fundamental issues of what counts as relevant knowledge and who has the right to determine what counts as relevant knowledge remain in the centre" (161). The results are significant: a body of research informed by other traditions as well as new ways of researching remains unavailable.

If the way we sponsor research is steeped in potentially exclusionary practices then so are the kinds of academic work valued and made available to scholars. This is not to criticize the necessity for evaluation or standards for different forms of promotion and professional reward. It is to recognize that publishing practices were created at a time when print, mail, and travel circumscribed the production and dissemination of work now done by many more people using a greater variety of theoretical bases, methods, and tools in a wider variety of contexts. Certainly today neither peer-reviewed journals nor scholarly monographs comprise the only—or even the primary—ways in which field-shaping data circulates. Instead, data that has defining influence on praxis, particularly in writing programs, is regularly found in programmatic or institutional materials comprised of planning documents, meeting minutes, handbooks and websites, teaching handouts, course projects, and unpublished findings. The research reported in these materials is often RAD or RFM work that provides a wealth of information to their initial audiences, even while the studies themselves remain inaccessible and therefore unknown to and uncitable by others. Unpublished research and the work it represents is often segregated from scholarship and scholarly conversations and, therefore, missing from most databases and bibliographies (which concentrate on published works). As a result, valuable and informative work is not counted or accounted for.

REx Responds

In 2006, as we began to imagine REx, Peter Smagorinsky's anthology, *Research on Composition: Multiple Perspectives on Two Decades of Change*, was published along with *The Handbook of Writing Research* by Charles A. MacArthur, Steve Graham, and Jill Fitzgerald. These have been joined on our bookshelves by a host of companion volumes, from the *Handbook of Research on Writing* (2009), edited by Charles Bazerman, to *Writing Studies Research in Practice* (2012), edited by Lee Nickoson and Mary P. Sheridan. This same period witnessed the inauguration of several new journals, including *The Journal of Writing Research*, and it saw the transformation of Santa Barbara's triennial international writing conferences into the International Society for the Advancement of Writing Research. During this same period, *CompPile* grew as a bibliographic resource, and the WAC Clearinghouse along with Parlor Press began publishing books and posting links to resources and program websites. Informed by these works and a combination of direct and indirect feedback from colleagues across the writing studies community, REx (as the Research Exchange) went through at least five major reinventions before emerging in 2011 as the Research Exchange Index. Throughout, the root goal of REx has remained the same: to improve our collective ability to conduct writing research by establishing a resource that promotes ongoing, accessible information exchange among writing researchers.

REx differs from existing resources in several important ways. A peer-built, peer-edited, and peer-reviewed resource, REx

- focuses on research processes along with research findings or products;
- provides summaries of research (as opposed to full-length articles);
- sorts information into searchable fields and categories;
- brings together information about completed, ongoing, and stalled studies.

Whereas scholarship tends to highlight research findings, REx collects information about the *activity* of research, starting with researchers' questions and the contexts for their work. REx also collects information about researchers' methods and methodologies, the logistics of individual projects, and both summaries of and reflections on completed as well as ongoing inquiries. REx also respects the fact that many researchers' regular professional interactions leave them little time or mental energy to spare; it asks only for summative descriptions of projects completed or in process. This information comes directly from researchers (see Figure 1). The contents of each report form the REx database and will be searchable by individual field and users' own key terms. This information will be available after a multistage process of collection, editing, and peer-review is complete and the database is formally published by a digital scholarly press.

On this calendar, the REx production process will take five to seven years, and once it is complete, production will begin again. That is to say, after the first edition of REx is published, information collection for REx, 2e will begin. At that time, researchers who reported projects in process will have an opportunity to update information about their work, while researchers with new projects will be able to register them. The second and all subsequent editions of REx will be cumulative, meaning REx users will be able to search all available editions both individually and together. In addition, we anticipate hosting a variety of related activities and publications, including workshops in REx best practices and publications that reflect what teachers and researchers learn when they put REx to use. Looking even further ahead and thinking about the ways in which available technologies may change and grow, we imagine the evolution of REx will only be limited by our collective imaginations—and our ability, as a community of practice, to match shared needs with sharable tools.

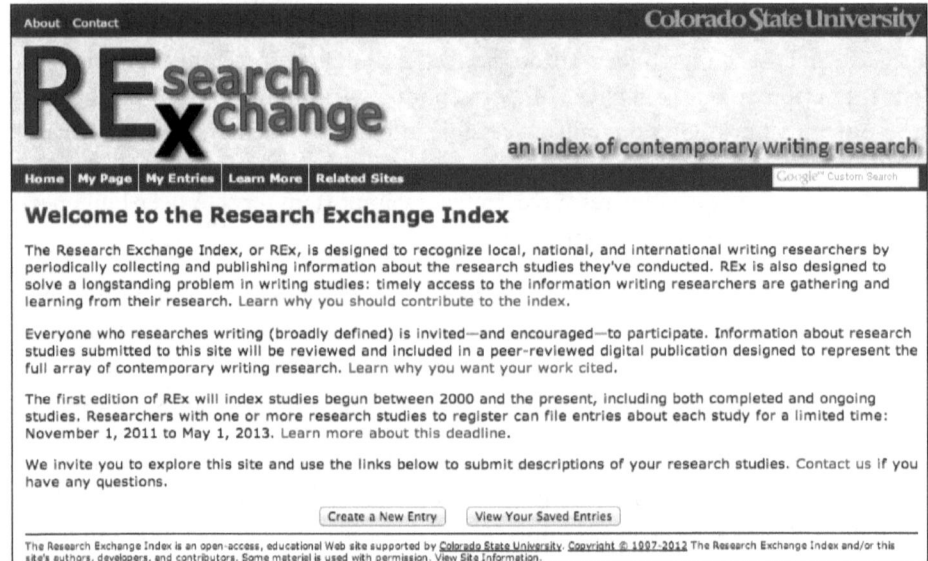

Figure 1. REx research report, accessible via the REx website, http://researchexchange.colostate.edu/.

Returning to the present, this essay marks the midway point in the REx production process. The first stage is taking place right now, and anyone who has conducted RAD or RFM research between 2000 and now should visit the REx website, establish an account, and file one report per individual project. Collection began at the National Council of Teachers of English Centennial Convention in November of 2011 and ends May 31, 2013. This phase of REx production is led by a group of more than thirty volunteers who serve as REx Acquisitions Editors (AEs). Located in and outside the U.S., AEs lead targeted collection efforts across writing studies' subfields, including assessment, basic writing, writing centers, digital composing, disability studies, discourse analysis, first-year composition, high school-to-college transition, K-12 writing, knowledge transfer, linguistics, second-language writing, teacher-research, technical and professional writing, two-year college writing research, WAC, and writing about writing. To cover these areas and others, AEs do their greatest work at conferences, talking face-to-face with current researchers. Through their efforts REx has been present at numerous 2011 and 2012 meetings, including the Conference on College Composition and Communication, Computers and Writing, the European Writing Center Association, the National Council of Teachers of English, and the Council of Writing Program Administrators, as well as the Research Network Forum, the International Writing Center Association Collaborative, and the Dartmouth Summer Seminar for Composition Research. In addition, AEs have directed their attention to regional conferences, informal meetings of local researchers, and individual departmental and program-based groups, and they have made good use of available digital resources.

As counterparts to AEs, Editorial Reviewers (ERs) will take over editorial responsibilities during the second phase of REx production, once acquisitions have ended, and they will focus on reviewing, fact checking, and copyediting reports to ensure their maximum usability. As editors, ERs will not serve as gatekeeper-critics, evaluating the design or execution of projects indexed in REx. Instead, ERs' responsibility will be to ensure the clarity and accuracy of the information contributors share about their research. To this end, as ERs work closely with subsets of REx contents, their goal will be to recommend individual reports for inclusion with or without revision. In some cases, reports may need only minor changes; in other cases reports may need greater corrections or clarifications. For example, ERs might ask contributors to define a specialized term, resolve conflicting chronological information, add further explanation to a project abstract or summary, or replace a dead link to online project findings. In addition, ERs will confirm that contributors have completed their reports, taking into account that each researcher may not have information for every item on the REx form. These activities will give ERs a unique perspective on database contents, and their final responsibility will be to file a short reflection on the materials they edited.

During stage two, we as managing editors will also read through the collected materials to complete work on framing the database with an introductory essay and glossary of research terms. Then, during stage three, we will submit the database and supporting materials to a digital scholarly press for peer review and publication. This somewhat attenuated process may seem unnecessary or extreme in an era of evolving scholarly communication, which includes proliferating wikis and increasingly sophisticated crowd-sourced scholarly publication. However, reception of earlier iterations of REx taught us the persistent importance and value of certain aspects of traditional publication, even as they confirmed the need for new kinds of resources. Thus, REx trades the gratification of instant access for a deliberately layered editorial process that will result in a resource that offers standardized content and a recognizably legitimate imprimatur (read: formally peer-reviewed, professionally published, and citable work).

Using REx to Change Research Practices and Access

Designed to be a comprehensive resource, REx makes easily visible our field's

- methodological diversity, embracing the many ways it is possible to design and carry out RAD and RFM research;
- geographic diversity, with participation from various collection sites and locations;
- theoretical diversity from multiple writing studies' subfields and writing researchers across disciplines.

Once REx is published it will promote multiple programmatic uses. For example, it will be possible to search REx reports for studies involving a particular methodology in order to explore its use over time. REx users might search the database to map features of hybrid research or track the influence of a particular theorist on inquiries conducted within a specific subfield during a set time. Likewise, researchers who come to REx hungry for practical information about program assessment will be able to quickly and easily identify relevant work, using either narrow searches through specific fields or keyword searches. Thus, researchers will be able to find examples conducted in similar institutions or on similar occasions (i.e., curriculum review, Quality Enhancement Program assessment, thesis project), and they will be able to narrow searches according to the location of data collection sites, institution types, and other shaping factors. Thanks in large part to the work of international AEs, REx may also make it possible to compare research practices and findings across international boundaries.

The REx database will also function as a rich teaching and mentoring tool for anyone offering courses in undergraduate or graduate research methods, leading professional development workshops for peers, or starting their own research career. For example:

- A new WAC director tasked with evaluating WAC courses in STEM departments uses REx to look up similar studies, something she can determine from a quick database search.
- A graduate researcher who has collected a large corpus of writing as part of his dissertation project is dissatisfied with the text analysis software he is using. He searches REx and finds reports that enable him to identify either better available analysis tools or better strategies for his particular study.

- After completing a site-based study that yields unexpected results, an experienced researcher goes to REx looking for others who reported similar findings. Although she does not find any, she does discover several studies that are similar to her own. She contacts the PIs and proposes pooling data in order to look for broader evidence of the phenomenon that so intrigued her.
- A new professor of writing studies is preparing a graduate seminar on WAC research. Teaching on the quarter system, she doesn't have time to assign full-fledged research projects. Instead she has her students mine REx for examples of research in different phases of completion. She also contacts individual researchers to find people willing to share process documents (IRB drafts and feedback, revised survey and interview protocols, etc.) and/or Skype into her class.
- A not-so-new professor of WAC is teaching a pre-dissertation seminar for doctoral students planning to conduct case study research for their dissertations. Using REx he finds strong examples of small studies similar to the work his students will be doing. In one or two cases, he even finds entries in which researchers have included descriptions of their projects from their original dissertation proposals.

As a teaching and mentoring resource, REx is thus not only a reservoir of static information but also a tool that promotes active communication among researchers, recognizing that everyone benefits from advice and guidance regardless of their level of experience or degree of training. At the same time, REx involves colleagues whose institutional affiliations (or non-affiliations) and rank, professional resources (or lack of resources), and/or research focus may isolate them from other researchers and relegate their contributions to the margins of formal scholarly conversations.

By creating a resource that is widely representative of contemporary writing research activity and application, REx is more than a practical tool that can make research easier and more efficient. REx also aims to change the culture of research in writing studies, especially for those who have "differential access to the global academic marketplace and the resources for full participation in it." REx ultimately asks all of us to "reimagine the kind of knowledge production, evaluation and distribution practices currently governing scholars' practices and experiences" (Lillis and Curry 155). Part of this reimagining, as Deborah Brandt observes, is responding as researchers to the way mass writing is replacing mass reading as the root of mass literacy (174). Scholarship on digital and multimodal composing is especially rich with observations about how writing now includes movie making, website building, and the self-designing and publishing of books. In this context, production and practice become more prominent and more closely associated with invention as well as agency. The time could not be more right for building REx, a resource that indexes information about the activity of research and promotes its exchange.

Joining other highly collaborative, digital native disciplinary resources such as Writing Spaces (http://writingspaces.org/), CompPile (http://www.comppile.org/) and The WAC Clearinghouse (http://http://wac.colostate.edu/), REx reflects the strength of our community's commitment to combined knowledge production and use. Similar to these resources, REx also lives and dies according to the quality of the writing studies community's participation. Most simply put, if researchers want what they say they want, those active between 2000 and the present must file reports about their work; if records of award-winning and often-cited studies are not indexed alongside records of unpublished and completed or ongoing research, then REx will be too limited in scope to be useful to anybody. REx may not be the most radical example of marshaling what Clay Shirky calls "cognitive surplus" (e.g., Wikipedia), yet it does demand widespread participation in resource creation. Perhaps it goes without saying that REx is an ambitious project, but it challenges our field to move beyond mere talk of inclusion and praxis by actively participating in new modes of scholarship and exchange: http://researchexchange.colostate.edu.

WORKS CITED

Ackerman, John M. "The Promise of Writing to Learn." *Written Communication* 10.3 (1993): 334–70. Web. 2 August 2012.

Babcock, Rebecca, and Terese Thonus. *Researching the Writing Center: Towards an Evidence-Based Practice*. New York: Peter Lang. 2012. Print.

Bazerman, Charles, ed. *Handbook of Research on Writing*. New York: Routledge, 2008. Print.

Brandt, Deborah. *Literacy and Learning: Reflections on Writing, Reading, and Society*. San Francisco: Jossey-Bass, 2009. Print.

Downs, Doug, and Elizabeth Wardle. "Teaching about Writing, Righting Misconceptions: (Re)Envisioning 'First-Year Composition' as 'Introduction to Writing Studies.'" *College Composition and Communication* 58.4 (June 2007): 552-84. Print.

Fulwiler, Toby. "Evaluating Writing Across the Curriculum Programs." *Strengthening Programs for Writing Across the Curriculum*. Ed. Susan McLeod. San Francisco: Jossey-Bass, 2000: 61-75. Web. 2 August 2012.

Haswell, Richard H. "Documenting Improvement in College Writing: A Longitudinal Approach." *Written Communication* 17.3 (July 2000): 307-52. Print.

—. "NCTE/CCCC's Recent War on Scholarship." *Written Communication* 22.1 (April 2005): 198-223. Print.

Lillis, Theresa, and Mary Jane Curry. *Academic Writing in a Global Context: The Politics and Practices of Publishing in English*. New York: Routledge. 2010. Print.

MacArthur, Charles A., Steve Graham, and Jill Fitzgerald, eds. *The Handbook of Writing Research.* New York: Guilford Press, 2006. Print.

Nickoson, Lee, and Mary P. Sheridan, eds. *Writing Studies Research in Practice: Methods and Methodologies.* Carbondale: Southern Illinois UP. 2012. Print.

Nowacek, Rebecca S. *Agents of Integration: Understanding Transfer as a Rhetorical Act.* Carbondale: Southern Illinois UP, 2012. Print.

Shirky, Clay. *Cognitive Surplus: Creativity and Generosity in a Connected Age.* New York: Penguin, 2010. Print.

Smagorinsky, Peter, ed. *Research on Composition: Multiple Perspectives on Two Decades of Change.* New York: Teachers College Press, 2005. Print.

Townsend, Martha. "WAC Program Vulnerability and What to Do About It: An Update and Brief Bibliographic Essay." *WAC Journal* 19 (Aug. 2008): 45-61. Web. 1 August 2012.

Crossing the Measurement and Writing Assessment Divide: The Practical Implications of Inter-Rater Reliability in Faculty Development

JENNIFER GOOD

I AM A HYBRID. With my terminal degree in educational psychology, which included a literacy cognate piecemealed from writing and pedagogy courses in both English and education, I live with one foot in the world of measurement and assessment and the other in the world of writing theory. Like Brian Huot (2009), whose "colleagues were concerned about hiring him because he had all this assessment stuff on his vita" (Huot & Dillon, p. 207), I have often felt that any efforts to provide quantifiable measures of writing assessment have been looked at with suspicion among my rhetoric and composition colleagues. This has created a tenuous balancing act for me. While I preach the power of the written word and understand its complexities and nuances, I also believe in the strength of numbers to document growth, change, and program value. As a result, my goal is to demonstrate how statistical analysis as part of an ongoing writing assessment can have practical benefits in a writing across the curriculum (WAC) program, specifically that of improving WAC faculty development offerings.

Because of my divided existence, I seek the marriage of writing assessment through authentic samples of student writing with quantifiable and psychometrically sound measurement methods. While I believe in the importance of writing measures that rely upon human raters who read and rate authentic writing samples in response to locally developed assignments (Conference on College Composition and Communication, 2009), I also believe it is essential to demonstrate the reliability of those measures, which means that any writing assignment that is rated, regardless of who completes the evaluation, will yield consistent scores. Thus, I present a model in use at my home university that demonstrates how an analysis of inter-rater reliability can be a bridge connecting the technical expectations of sound psychometric properties in measurement with assessment of authentic writing samples. Through this model, I also demonstrate how the results can be used to suggest practical ongoing reform for WAC faculty development at both the group and individual levels.

Colleagues of mine in the composition program have told me that they "don't do numbers." Trusting their own expertise in writing pedagogy and theory, they feel confident that the feedback they provide on student papers is sound, fair, and equitable. O'Neill and Moore (2009) explain that most college professors recognize the social, contextualized nature of writing and, in an effort to protect that understanding, resist any measure that minimizes writing achievement to mere numbers: "Misfires can happen in writing assessment when tests are not sensitive to the particular students and their contexts" (p. 37). Like O'Neill and Moore, I value the importance of individual feedback and response to student writing, yet this realization does not make the development of common writing assessments with proven psychometric properties an easy task to accomplish. O'Neill and Moore continue their argument by stating the following: "Because of its complexity, writing cannot be researched—or measured—in the same way that physical traits such as height or weight might be measured" (p. 40).

In his historical overview of writing assessment, Condon (2010) chronicles the trends and changes that have occurred over the past decades, from debates and arguments about the actual measurement tool to issues of reliability and validity. He criticizes initiatives sparked by writing theorists that describe "concepts such as validity and reliability as hegemonic forces of the commercial enterprises that inevitably undermine attempts to establish better assessments" (p. 176). In response, Condon promotes the importance of statistics and sound measurement practices in this ongoing debate, while also emphasizing the need for authentic and contextualized writing production through meaningful prompts and assignments. In agreement with Condon, I feel it is important to create and find models to balance sound measurement with writing samples produced in response to discipline-specific assignments and problems. A number of other writing assessment theorists have emerged in this ongoing conversation (Gallagher, 2010; Huot, 1996), also extolling the benefits of considering properties such as reliability and validity when measuring authentic writing samples. Huot and Dillon (2009) provide the following summative argument: "Writing teachers and program administrators should make an effort to become more familiar with the terminology and beliefs of educational measurement" (p. 216).

Acknowledging that "good writing is a complex process that varies by discipline" (Brockman, Taylor, Crawford, & Kreth, 2010), it can be assumed that good assessment of writing is equally as complex, particularly for faculty from different disciplines, with different levels of expertise regarding writing pedagogy and writing assessment. In response to the need to measure authentic writing samples with a degree of consistency, rubrics are often offered as a solution, as they capture writing outcomes at various levels of performance (Spandel, 2006). Yet, even though a rubric may measure writing skills at various stages of competencies, an abundance of types of writing rubrics and scoring guides exist, and selecting or understanding the use of a particular rubric as it aligns appropriately with an assignment becomes necessary for effective writing instruction (Moskal, 2000).

Even when using rubrics or other scoring guides, Stern (2009) notes that comments regarding assessment of writing samples varied. Leckie and Baird (2011) argue that many factors, including rater severity, rater expertise, and central tendency of a rater can create bias and variation in writing assessment. They noted that rater severity in particular was unstable and changed over time. According to writing experts, administrators must "consider whether we are studying what we think we are studying and whether the measures we use are consistent" (Writing @CSU Guide). In response to the importance of reliability, the training and follow-up statistical model that I have incorporated as part of our regular WAC program operations allows for open discussion of the effect raters can have on evaluation, recognizing that, ethically, the consistency of writing evaluation must be determined when used in high-stakes decision-making or in overall writing program evaluation.

Because a primary aim of many university-wide WAC programs is to ensure that students improve in writing outcomes, consistent assessment of writing and understanding for faculty in all disciplines of the characteristics or dimensions of effective writing becomes imperative. For this reason, inter-rater reliability, or the degree of agreement among two or more raters based upon the relationship in their scores, is often considered. This is not to imply that the students should write in response to common university-wide assignments using the same organizational and stylistic expectations in every class regardless of discipline. Rather, the raters of the students' writing should have some common understanding of the complex components or dimensions of writing that they evaluate, which can then be considered at a discipline-specific level. An analysis of intra-class correlation, which means how closely individual ratings resemble each other within a group, can be used to determine overall inter-rater reliability when using a rubric or scoring guide. What makes this model unique, however, is the follow-up emphasis on individual interclass ratings, or the single measure of one set of ratings to another individual set of ratings within a group. In the case of this model, I use my ratings—as both facilitator of faculty development and program administrator who is responsible for bringing a comprehensive unification to the program goals—as the point of reference or expertise for assessing individual faculty member rubric ratings. Because I compare faculty ratings to my own ratings, two primary benefits emerge when adopting this statistical approach to inter-rater reliability: (a) the first consideration of data can improve group training materials and emphasis of training that is designed and facilitated by me; and (b) the second consideration of data can suggest follow-up training at the individual faculty level to continue to allow me to provide ongoing support to help faculty members understand the university's WAC program and its learning outcomes. This article provides a faculty professional development model that integrates a statistical analysis to help inform further reform in faculty training. The model presented can be easily adapted for use at other institutions.

The Training Model: Connecting Numbers and Words

Before a statistical analysis of ratings can occur, ratings must be collected, and it is within the WAC program faculty development sessions that I have faculty generate these. Our WAC program, and the faculty training integral to the program's success, were developed in response to our accrediting agency's requirement of a quality enhancement plan. For this reason, the program had the support of both administration and faculty in its early stages of design. The content-area faculty at my institution engage in 30 hours of extensive professional development to prepare them for and support them in writing-intensive instruction; these professional development hours are spread throughout 10 sessions over two academic semesters. According to our WAC program procedures, training is required and provided each semester to faculty members who are interested in teaching writing-intensive, content-area courses from different disciplines. Because the program is highly incentivized by the university administration, including $100 per training session that is transferred into appropriate departmental accounts for individual use and the potential of a course release for research after teaching three writing-intensive courses, it is a popular program. Approximately one third of our tenured or tenure-track faculty members, representing all departments and academic schools, have participated within the past three years.

The first four sessions of faculty training, offered prior to writing-intensive instruction, focus on overall program goals and procedures, including the writing assessment requirements that measure student learning outcomes and inform the program's development. It is within the third session, after the WAC program's objectives have been discussed in this faculty development model, that writing assessment methods are shared in detail. An informal inter-rater reliability exercise is included within the session. Although no statistical analysis of the ratings provided by faculty occurs at this point, this exercise allows for an introductory discussion among faculty of the five unique writing dimensions that are collected and measured within the WAC program's assessment system to measure student outcomes of writing growth.

As defined by common university-wide objectives and fleshed out in a university-wide rubric, these five dimensions are *Focus, Content, Organization, Style*, and

Language Conventions. Training first introduces content-area faculty to these five dimensions of writing and, after establishment of common understandings of terms and expectations per dimension, discussions of the unique indicators that help to define each dimension at the discipline level also ensue. Although I will be providing sample ratings and correlations on each of these dimensions, it is important to note that *the method* of assessing and analyzing the rubric, more so than the actual rubric, is the centerpiece of this model.

When completing the first inter-rater reliability activity in the third session of training, faculty members must grapple with the meaning of good writing as it aligns with the university's writing program objectives as well as their specific discipline expectations. In order to do that, they read and evaluate three different student-generated written products, rating each of the three products on each dimension of the rubric. The three written products are all in response to a single persuasive prompt and have been intentionally selected to present weak, acceptable, and exceptional writing on a number of the writing dimensions.

After completing the evaluation, the ratings per faculty member are revealed and shared, allowing individuals to defend, question, and discuss the ratings they provided; the faculty members are asked to use specific indicators within each writing dimension and language from the rubric template to support their points during the discussion. This initial interaction with the university's rubric opens conversations that help develop faculty members' understandings of the complexities of writing and some of the difficulties of writing assessment, such as rater bias, or raters' judgments and perceptions that cloud their evaluation of writing, and severity, which means the tendency of some raters to be harsh or lenient relative to other raters.

The final six sessions of professional development occur simultaneously with the faculty member's first semester of writing-intensive instruction, with one session each dedicated to allowing faculty to discuss and understand a different writing dimension within the rubric. During each of these sessions, faculty members closely study the indicators that define each of the writing dimensions being assessed for the university-wide writing program. Views and definitions of each dimension are demanded and challenged through prompts and discussion boards, while instructional strategies that can be used in the classroom to help students improve in a particular dimension are offered, generating thoughts on instructional strategies and feedback to help the faculty members move from the rubric ratings to improvement of writing at the individual student level. In these sessions, faculty members are asked to refine the indicators that define each rubric dimension to help them tease out their own discipline-specific expectations.

In the sixth session of the second part of training, faculty members are asked to participate in a second inter-rater reliability exercise. Unlike the first inter-rater reliability experience, this final rating activity occurs at the end of a full semester of writing-intensive instruction and at the completion of intensive in-depth consideration of both the writing dimensions and the indicators that inform and define each of the dimensions. Because the faculty members have practiced using the rubric in response to authentic writing samples generated in their classes, they are able to hold deeper conversations than offered in the initial introductory sessions regarding assessment. The data from this exercise are collected and analyzed each semester.

After the completion of the final faculty training session and the collection of outcome ratings, inter-rater reliability is determined, and an inter-item correlation matrix is created. As the university's WAC program director, I first look at intra-class correlation coefficients, selected over Cronbach's alpha due to the statistical analyses' ability to tease out complexities such as interaction effect which strengthen the consideration of the extent to which the raters agree, per each of the analytic rubric's writing dimensions; these intra-class correlation coefficients per dimension are analyzed to establish overall technical merit of the university's rubric. I then consider interclass correlation coefficients, or the relationship of one rater to another rater using my ratings, to help determine the individual faculty members who may need additional support in understanding and completing assessments and ratings that are consistent with the university's expectations. Because the director of the program facilitates the faculty training in alignment with the WAC program objectives, I decided to use my ratings for comparison against the individual faculty ratings that are generated in the correlation matrix, as I will also be the facilitator of follow-up training.

The Model in Action: Two Semesters of Lessons Learned

For the initial analysis of inter-rater reliability, five of us rated six unique essays on a scale of 1 (*Inadequate*) to 5 (*Excellent*) per each of the five writing dimensions of the rubric. This initial cohort included me, the WAC senior program associate, and three faculty members from departments in three of the five academic schools on campus: Liberal Arts, Sciences, and Education. For this first analysis of data, I asked each of the faculty members to submit two anonymous and brief writing samples collected during their first semester of writing-intensive content-area instruction, one perceived as a sample of strong or effective writing and the other perceived as a sample of weak writing in their disciplines.

During the first data collection for inter-rater reliability, the overall intra-class correlation coefficients per writing dimension appeared sufficient, as noted by .70 alpha levels or higher, and demonstrated the writing rubric's reliability (Focus=.83; Content=.71; Organization=.81; Style=.80; Language Conventions=.70). Practically speaking, however, the overall intra-class correlation coefficient tells us little to nothing helpful in terms of improving an individual faculty member's ability to assess writing dimensions with consistency relative to other faculty members. It is this consistency of raters we seek in order to have common understanding of expectations and outcomes across the entire university. How can these data regarding an individual's rater reliability be teased out of the available data that is generated during this professional development exercise? As a follow-up step, I considered each individual faculty members' ratings per dimension and looked for differences from my ratings in each dimension to discover where rating issues may exist. Table 1 provides the intra-class correlation coefficients, or the similarity of individuals within a group to determine ratings, using my ratings for comparison purposes.

Table 1. Inter-item correlation coefficients between expert rater and faculty training participants

	Focus	Content	Organization	Style	Language Conventions
Rater 1	.343	.000	.200	-.108	.791
Rater 2	.691	.698	.586	.412	.421
Rater 3	.343	-.185	.067	.108	.281
Rater 4	.788	.982	.890	.692	.750

The relationship of individual faculty members' rating scores to my rating scores was disappointing in this first iteration of data collection. For instance, using .70 as an acceptable correlation coefficient, only Rater 4 appeared to be consistent in her ratings per dimension with mine, yielding positive and strong correlation coefficients. Both Rater 1 and Rater 3 actually had negative correlation coefficients on at least one of the dimensions in comparison to my ratings, which means that these two raters were actually moving in opposite directions from my ratings (i.e., if my rating increased for a dimension, their ratings would decrease). Faculty comments at the completion of this exercise supported the data showing a lack of understanding of certain dimensions on the rubric, as faculty noted that evaluating writing samples from disciplines outside of their areas of expertise was difficult, particularly in the writing dimensions of *Content* and *Style*. The data from the analysis supported and confirmed their verbalized concerns. The inconsistency of the ratings between me and most of the faculty suggests that I need to revise some of the professional development sessions and emphasize a better understanding of what we are actually measuring and evaluating related to content or style in student writing. These two dimensions were not consistent in rating responses, nor did they match my understanding, as the writing program administrator, of the dimensions. The most important kernel of wisdom that I gleaned from this initial analysis was that the acceptable overall reliability coefficients for each dimension (range of .70 to .83), although sufficient by textbook standards, were not sufficient when trying to understand the individual needs and understanding of faculty members from different disciplines. Some faculty members simply were not in alignment with me or other members of the university when rating student writing, which, if not addressed, could potentially limit the success of the WAC program overall.

These disappointing individual inter-item correlation coefficients prompted the need for change. Specifically, although faculty members again provided two anonymous samples that had not yet been rated, the following areas were addressed for the next cohort of faculty undergoing training: (a) I required sample length of three pages or less to encourage brevity for the inter-rater reliability exercise in the final training session; (b) Because the majority of disagreement and debate during discussion centered around defining ratings of 3 in the rubric continuum, instead of requesting weak and strong writing samples, I asked the faculty members to provide papers they considered to be 3-rated on the majority of the writing dimensions, as well as one that was primarily 5-rated, and the six new writing samples were selected from among these papers; and (c) I requested the actual writing assignment handout of instructions to accompany the writing sample in order to help the faculty engaged in rating papers to understand the focus, purpose, and criteria of the assignment as defined by the instructors.

After making these programmatic changes to the faculty training, the final rating activity and statistical analysis was repeated with 11 faculty members who were completing training in the next semester of writing-intensive instruction; these faculty members represented seven departments or disciplines within the Schools of Business, Liberal Arts, and Sciences. With the change in emphases in both instruction during professional development and its impact on the final inter-rater reliability exercise, the second round of data generated revealed improvement in understanding of and consistency in rating the dimensions of writing. Intra-class correlation coefficients increased for all five dimensions of the writing rubric (Focus=.94; Content=.94; Organization=.95; Style=.93; Language Conventions=.93). Because of the improved coefficients on this second analysis of data, I now continue to use those same writing samples, which represent three different academic disciplines, with all new training cohorts, enabling me to analyze data across an entire year and make longitudinal decisions about program improvement.

In spite of the improvement in intra-class correlation, a consideration of the inter-item correlation coefficients from the faculty member to my ratings revealed a need for additional revision to faculty training. For instance, if using a .70 coefficient as a goal for consistency in ratings from the individual faculty member to my ratings, only one faculty member, Rater 3, achieved acceptable reliability ratings on all five writing dimensions (see Table 2.) Possibly, for future and follow-up training, this faculty member could act as an additional facilitator of professional development or a mentor for other faculty members, particularly within her discipline, as faculty continue to grapple with and learn about the writing program and the program's stated objectives and expectations of student writing.

Table 2. Inter-item correlation coefficients between expert rater and faculty training participants

	Focus	Content	Organization	Style	Language Conventions
Rater 1	.657	.463	.354	.768	.722
Rater 2	.853	.271	.802	.674	.459
Rater 3	.945	.793	.913	.768	.702
Rater 4	.316	.492	.267	.598	.702
Rater 5	.853	.800	.956	.676	.631
Rater 6	.433	.836	.433	.559	.411
Rater 7	.866	.800	.500	.632	.791
Rater 8	.739	.922	.491	.860	.770
Rater 9	.426	.768	.640	.586	.884
Rater 10	.632	.812	.673	.950	.702
Rater 11	.562	.897	.682	.632	.554

Diagnostically, these data can be used to inform more changes to the professional development program. For instance, a global overview per writing dimension reveals that the *Content* and *Language Convention* dimensions yielded the most consistency in ratings per individual participants to my ratings, suggesting that faculty have a common understanding of these dimensions, which allows them to rate writing samples in these areas reliably. In contrast, when looking at the correlation coefficients for *Organization* and *Style*, only Raters 3 and 4 of the 11 faculty members rated in close relationship to my ratings (at .70 coefficient or above), intimating that these two writing dimensions need further attention in group training to support faculty members' understanding of the elements or indicators that define these particular dimensions.

What is most beneficial is that the data helps all faculty members understand that additional faculty development can be helpful as they continue to navigate writing-intensive instruction in their disciplines. For instance, Rater 4 yields consistently low inter-item correlation coefficients when compared to my ratings, from a range of .267 to .702. This finding intimates that I need to give additional attention and individualized instruction to Rater 4. For instance, informal sessions that allow co-rating of other papers could open conversations and discussion about interpretations of the dimensions in the rubric, possibly confronting misunderstandings or deepening knowledge of writing elements. In other cases, the matrix of data suggests that I may want to discuss only one or two dimensions of the rubric with the faculty member. For instance, Rater 5 has strong inter-item correlation coefficients on three of the writing dimensions; however, *Style* and *Language Convention*s tend to be more problematic. Similarly, Rater 8 has strong inter-item correlation coefficients when compared to my ratings on everything except *Organization*.

This matrix of correlation coefficients acts as a map of individual needs for the faculty members at the conclusion of the program. The intent of this analysis is not to point out individual weaknesses of faculty in understanding writing elements or in their ability to rate reliably. Rather, the point of the analysis is to seek areas to focus support in faculty development. The data inform me about overall faculty program success as well as individual faculty who may need more attention or assistance.

To date, the faculty members have been responsive to informal follow-up requests to meet and discuss the rubric, assessment methods, and assignments as a result of this analysis. When first introducing the activity during training, some faculty members have expressed concern over publicly sharing and discussing their ratings, fearing they would be embarrassed if they didn't align with other faculty members. They also indicated that they didn't want ratings that may reflect their performance in the WAC program, particularly if ratings were not in alignment with other faculty, to get shared with departmental administrators who complete faculty performance evaluations. I had to ensure that the individual ratings would remain inside the WAC program and would not be shared with administrators for any personnel evaluative purpose. Because I have remained true to this promise, faculty members have learned to trust the professional development benefits of the inter-rater reliability experience. Due mostly to open communication in the previous nine sessions within the cohort, they accept that the objective of the inter-rater reliability activity, in alignment with the overall faculty development experience, is to enhance their ability to teach and assess writing in their discipline-specific courses, not to judge or rate them as teachers.

At the end of the full training experience, faculty members are asked to provide anonymous written responses and feedback regarding training. The prompts ask that they consider training program strengths, weaknesses, and topics for future training sessions. Other than comments requesting more emphasis on how to teach online writing-intensive courses, the feedback regarding the training experience was positive. Sample comments from these final evaluations parallel my perception of the content-area faculty members' willingness to continue to grow and learn in writing pedagogy and assessment:

- I would like to see more on grading strategies.
- More opportunities to assess writing in training before we actually implement our writing-intensive course.
- I'd like to see us have more work and discussion on inter-rater reliability.
- The strengths include focusing on peer review, evaluating using the assessment rubric, sharing classroom problems and experiences, and focusing on kinds of writing assignments that we can give.
- A strength is bonding and learning with other faculty across disciplines. I loved it and learned so much about how to collaboratively learn with professionals in multiple disciplines.
- Working with other faculty to compare and contrast was a strength.

Having the opportunity to share their ratings on student-produced writing assignments from colleagues' discipline-specific classes and discuss and defend the ratings they provided in training created an opportunity for interdisciplinary growth and teamwork.

Conclusions

By looking at the inter-item correlation coefficients per individual faculty member and comparing them to my own, I am better able to ascertain which faculty members continue to struggle with specific writing dimensions. In essence, the matrix becomes my blueprint that enables me to communicate individually with a faculty member and provide additional support or practice in evaluating writing samples on specific writing dimensions. Essentially, the benefits of individual conferencing with students regarding their papers can be modeled with faculty when I individually conference with them regarding their writing assessment.

Certainly, checking the psychometric properties of a writing rubric, such as validity and reliability, is valuable for any program that uses a rubric to measure growth in student outcomes. Yet, on a practical level, many administrators and trainers stop at the first broad sweep of the data when they feel it has produced sufficient results. Few bother to look at the data at a deeper level and consider the story it tells about the various faculty training components of the writing program and what it reveals about the need for additional follow-up in faculty training, both at the group level and the individual faculty member level.

The inclusion of a regular check of reliability for the writing rubric used at my institution developed into a more detailed overview of reliability at the individual faculty level, which then created an abundance of ideas for reforming faculty training and a mechanism for identifying individual faculty members who may need more support and assistance. From research and regular analysis of reliability of writing rubrics, administrators can prompt action and revision in the practical world of faculty training. The practical implications discovered through rigorous analysis of inter-rater reliability can improve both faculty understanding of good writing and faculty development offerings.

REFERENCES

Brockman, E., Taylor, M., Crawford, M. K., & Kreth, M. (2010). Helping students cross the threshold: Implications from a university writing assessment. *English Journal, 99*(3), 42-50.

Condon, W. (2010). Reinventing writing assessment: How the conversation is shifting. *WPA: Writing Program Administration, 34*(2), 162-82.

Conference on College Composition and Communication. (2009, March). *Writing assessment: A position statement* (Rev. ed.). Retrieved from http://www.ncte.org/cccc/resources/positions/writingassessment

Gallagher, C. W. (2010). Assess locally, validate globally: Heuristics for validating local writing assessments. *WPA: Writing Program Administration, 34*(1), 10-32.

Huot, B. (1996). Toward a new theory of writing assessment. *College Composition and Communication, 47*, 549-66.

Huot, B., & Dillon, E. (2009). WAC and writing program assessment take another step: A response to Assessment of Writing. In M. C. Paretti & K. M. Powell (Eds.). *Assessment of Writing* (pp. 207-18). Tallahassee, FL: Association for Institutional Research.

Leckie, G., & Baird, J. (2011). Rater effects on essay scoring: A multilevel analysis of severity drift, central tendency, and rater experience. *Journal of Educational Measurement, 48*, 399-418.

Moskal, B. M. (2000). Scoring rubrics: What, when, and how? *Practical Assessment, Research and Evaluation, 7*(3). Retrieved July 15, 2011 from http://goo.gl/ep8pe

O'Neill, P., & Moore, C. (2009). What college writing teachers value and why it matters. In M.C. Paretti & K. M. Powell (Eds.), *Assessment of Writing* (pp. 35-47). Tallahassee, FL: Association for Institutional Research.

Spandel, V. A. (2006). In defense of rubrics, *English Journal, 96*(1) 19-22.

Stern, L. A. (2006). Effective faculty feedback: The road less traveled. *Assessing Writing, 11*, 22-41.

Writing@CSU. (2012). Reliability and validity. Colorado State University. Retrieved 19 June 2012 from http://writing.colostate.edu/guides/research/relval/pop2a.cfm

Articulating Claims and Presenting Evidence: A Study of Twelve Student Writers, From First-Year Composition to Writing Across the Curriculum

J. PAUL JOHNSON & ETHAN KRASE

IN RECENT DECADES, composition studies has directed increased attention to the ways that students' writing in first-year composition (FYC) prepares them for their later writing across the curriculum (WAC). Recent scholarship has worked to identify the characteristics and contexts common to literacy development as students progress from FYC to WAC. Among the rhetorical skills most critical to students' disciplinary writing is the ability to construct effective arguments (Graff, 2003; Hillocks, 2010, 2011). This longitudinal study examines the transfer of a key component of argumentation—the ability to articulate claims and support them with evidence—from FYC to WAC in the junior and senior years.

A number of longitudinal studies (Herrington, 1984; McCarthy, 1987; Walvoord & McCarthy, 1990; Herrington & Curtis, 2000; Carroll, 2002; Theiss & Zawicki, 2006; and Beaufort, 2007) examine the complexities of transferring skills and abilities from FYC to later work across the curriculum. Among the core findings in this body of work are, first, that the development of writing ability during the college years does not come easily, and, second, that the notion of *transfer* is central to student growth between FYC and WAC. Indeed, as Smit (2004) suggests, "The ability to transfer knowledge and ability from one context to another is *what we mean by learning in the first place*" (p. 130, emphasis added). The transfer of writing skills from one context to another is often unpredictable: such transfer "depends on the learners' background and experience, factors over which teachers have little control" (Smit, 2004, p. 119). When transfer does occur, it comes about because learners "see the similarity between what they have learned in the past and what they need to do in new contexts" (Smit, 2004, p. 119). In order, then, for students to transfer skills beyond FYC and into WAC, they must be prepared and encouraged to do so.

Researchers have only recently begun to examine, more specifically, the transfer of argument skills from FYC into WAC. In a pilot study presenting self-reported comments from seven student writers as they moved from FYC into their first two years of WAC, Wardle (2007) found that skills do not transfer unless students "*perceive a need* to adopt or adapt most of the writing behaviors they used in FYC for other courses" (Wardle's emphasis, p. 76). In their study of two student writers' formation of claims during their first year of study in both FYC and WAC, Greene and Orr (2007) conclude that the substantive differences in the two domains force students to adapt strategies learned in FYC in order to maximize their utility across the curriculum.

Such adaptation is seldom simple. Fukuzawa and Boyd (2008) note that students frequently struggle as they begin WAC, in large part because they do not always understand clearly the writing requirements they face beyond FYC. For a variety of reasons, direct transfer of writing skill from one context (such as FYC) to another (such as WAC) is unlikely; only certain "portable" skills may be accessible to students as they move into their major fields of study (Smit, 2004; Dias et al., 1999). To become truly adept, students must develop recognition of their fields as coherent collections of diverse perspectives in which they themselves must advance their own arguments (Thaiss and Zawacki, 2006). These complexities underscore Rose's (1989) "myth of transience"—the belief that writing skills can be learned completely in a single class or as a simple result of a prescribed course of action. For students to become successful, capable writers instead requires a protracted period of time during which they encounter many opportunities to write and receive feedback in multiple contexts.

To better understand the complexities of this transfer of argumentation skills, we examined the work of twelve student writers as they transitioned from FYC to their later WAC, ranging from traditional liberal arts to education, nursing, and science. Our analysis is based on Toulmin's (1958/2003) broad formulation of argument and its emphasis on claims and evidence. Toulmin's model begins with what he called the *claim*, the main point a writer hopes to assert. A claim, whether of fact, policy, or value, is then supported by *evidence* (what Toulmin called the *data*). Evidence may take the form of examples, statistics, testimony, and/or analogy; evidence may be offered in different forms, quantities, or combinations, depending upon the rhetorical situation. Toulmin's model also accounts for *qualification*: such may include, for instance, exceptions which limit the strength of the claim or its evidence. The other elements of Toulmin's model—such as its *warrants* (what the reader must believe in order to agree that the evidence supports the claim), *backing* (evidence provided in support of the warrant), and *rebuttals*—convey the nuances of an argument more so than its basic structure, which can be seen primarily in its claims and evidence.

Toulmin's taxonomy of argument allows for accommodation of the generic features of argument, primarily its use of claims and evidence, across multiple disciplinary areas. With it, we set out to address the following: Did students employ claims in their writing in FYC and WAC? Were students' claims clear, concise and qualified? Did students support claims with authoritative, varied, and documented evidence? As students progressed through and beyond FYC to WAC in their various undergraduate majors, did their abilities to employ claims and evidence improve?

Methods

Our study was conducted at a comprehensive Midwestern public four-year university requiring a single four-credit FYC course. Taught by a range of instructors, from teaching assistants to adjunct, temporary, full-time, and tenured faculty, FYC includes a significant reading component, typically culminating in a substantial source-based argumentative research project. Beyond FYC exists a WAC requirement, where students complete at least two, and frequently more, such courses, typically in their selected majors.

The students whose work is examined here are selected from a subset of those who had participated in an earlier study of FYC. The earlier study began with a statistically random sampling of FYC students (n=1501); the subset from which these students were selected was limited to those who had continued their college careers at the same institution, who were completing a declared major, and who expressed a willingness to participate. Participants were offered a $50 gift card to the university bookstore in exchange for their participation. Twelve students completed the full round of activities related to the study; their participation was voluntary and solicited in full cooperation with IRB regulations.

In order to examine more closely the individual students' transition from FYC to their later WAC coursework, we collected and triangulated data from multiple sources and at various stages of development. The earlier study provided source-based argument papers and performance assessments from students' FYC classes: students composed two source-based papers, written in response to similar prompts, near both the beginning and the conclusion of FYC. These were later evaluated in a double-blind scoring session by trained raters.[1] Portfolios of WAC projects were then collected from each participant, including written papers that employed systems of claims and their supporting evidence. The participants reviewed the work they had composed and selected five or six representative samples of their writing as indicated in Table 1.

---

1. After a pilot scoring and subsequent training session, inter-rater reliability for the final essay scoring was 97%. In those few instances where the two raters diverged, a third rater adjudicated.

Table 1. Writing across the curriculum genres. Projects requiring systems of claims and evidence are listed in italics.

Participant	Major	Genres in Major Field
Amy	Public Relations	news writing, feature writing, *research reports*, performance reviews, *analytical papers*
Claire	Pre-Law	*argumentation (in preparation for senior thesis), legal briefs and reports*
Evan	Pre-Law	*argumentation (in preparation for senior thesis), legal briefs and reports*
Hailey	Nursing	care plans, discharge summaries, health pamphlets, annotated bibliographies, *literature reviews, research reports*
Kate	Biology	*science lab reports, case studies, literature reviews*
Lois	Psychology	*research reports, letters to legislators*
Melanie	Business Education	*persuasive writing, case studies, research summaries,* lesson plans, autobiographies, *teaching philosophy statements*
Nikki	Health Promotion	*literature reviews, empirical research,* health pamphlets, *research essays*
Rita	Advertising	*literature reviews, self-assessments, empirical research,* media plans
Mary	TESOL/Spanish Education	*research papers, empirical research, literature reviews,* annotated bibliographies, lesson plans, *teaching philosophy statements*
Sheryl	Nursing	care plans, discharge summaries, health pamphlets, reflective journal entries, *outcomes statements, literature reviews, research reports*
Steve	Composite Engineering	*engineering lab reports*, shop orders

Student writing culled from these portfolios provides the primary data source for this analysis. Since few transfer studies present data from actual student discourse (as opposed to self-reported behaviors, e.g., Wardle, 2007), our analysis focuses nearly exclusively on the writing conducted in students' FYC and WAC coursework. Each student's portfolio provided the opportunity to examine student writing at three specific data points:

1. First-Year Composition, Start of Term
2. First-Year Composition, End of Term
3. Writing Across the Curriculum

While students' portfolios included multiple samples of WAC, we limited our analysis to a single representative paper composed for an upper-division course. In all instances, student portfolios included at least one such paper that employed claims and evidence comparable to those produced in FYC. Using the results of the double-blind review conducted in the earlier study of FYC, we compared the set of WAC papers with each student's FYC work, in the process examining the following:

- *Claims*: Did the work feature discernible claims, and to what degree or extent?
- *Concision*: Were claims concise, or did they suffer from wordiness?
- *Clarity*: Were claims clear, or did they suffer from imprecision or ambiguity?
- *Qualification*: Were claims appropriately qualified?
- *Support*: Were claims supported with evidence, such as example, testimony, or fact?
- *Evidence*: Was evidence employed from researched sources or limited to personal experience?
- *Documentation*: Was evidence from sources acknowledged according to a recognized format (such as MLA, APA, CSE, etc.)?

The small sample size precludes us from making generalizations about any group of students beyond the twelve participating in this study. Additionally, we recognize that any single paper may be less than perfectly indicative of a student's ability. However, the papers selected for the analysis were volunteered by the students as representative of their recent work. Close analysis of multiple works produced by each student at three distinct moments in their undergraduate careers further allows for a considerable degree of familiarity with each individual sample of student writing and the overall work of each student in particular. In our analysis of the data, we witnessed a number of discernible patterns—both for individual students and for the group of them collectively—that suggest implications for student learning in general and WAC in particular.

Results

The study's twelve participants are identified by pseudonyms to preserve their anonymity. Table 2, Evaluation of Claims and Evidence, lists each participant's pseudonym and paper topics. Additionally indicated is each student's degree of success in employing claims and evidence in a specific paper at the three aforementioned data points, labeled as **1 FYC** (start of term), **2 FYC** (end of term) and **3 WAC**.

Table 2. Evaluation of claims and evidence.

Amy	topic	claims	concision	clarity	qualification	support	evidence	documentation	notes
FYC 1	abstinence-only education	●	O	O	O	O	●	O	claims present in each ¶ but with pervasive problems
FYC 2	public smoking ban	●	●	●	●	●	●	●	improved claims and use of evidence in every respect
WAC 3	Egypt's press freedom	●	●	●	●	O	O	●	no improvement; claims exist but often unsupported

Claire	topic								notes
FYC 1	teen driving	O	O	O	O	O	O	O	all claims & evidence focused on self, no evidence in support
FYC 2	school uniforms	●	●	●	O	●	●	●	developing use of claims, but overreliance on "self" for evidence
WAC 3	treatment of juvenile offenders	●	●	●	●	●	●	✱	little improvement other than qualification, documentation

Evan	topic								notes
FYC 1	sex and media	O	O	O	O	O	O	O	claims present but reasoning is simplistic, circular, naïve
FYC 2	Patriot Act	●	●	O	O	O	O	●	more concise, precise claims; evidence sometimes irrelevant
WAC 3	insanity defense	O	●	●	O	O	●	✱	"encyclopedia style" prevents true claim + development

Hailey	topic								notes
FYC 1	minimum wage	O	O	O	O	●	●	●	claims exist, yet lack concision and clarity; evidence is useful
FYC 2	illegal immigration	●	●	●	●	✱	●	✱	claims more clear, precise; good sense of support/use of evidence
WAC 3	preeclampsia	●	●	✱	✱	✱	●	✱	evidence limited to one source per paragraph; claims still wordy

Kate	topic								notes
FYC 1	parenting	●	●	O	●	O	●	O	claims always present, sometimes lacking clarity
FYC 2	global food market	✱	✱	✱	✱	✱	✱	O	clear claims with excellent supporting evidence
WAC 3	garlic variations	✱	✱	✱	✱	✱	✱	✱	consistently effective claims supported by researched evidence

Lois	topic								notes
FYC 1	education	●	O	●	O	O	O	O	claims clear & conspicuous, but also naïve and lacking concision
FYC 2	9/11 conspiracies	✱	●	●	●	O	●	●	improved claims yet continued difficulties with support
WAC 3	eating disorders	✱	✱	✱	✱	✱	✱	✱	concise claims with varied researched evidence as support

Mary	topic								notes
FYC 1	vegetarianism	●	✱	✱	●	O	●	O	claims are reasonable, supported; no use of documentation
FYC 2	bilingual education	✱	✱	✱	●	●	●	●	improved claims and stronger evidence throughout
WAC 3	memory/recall & L2 FYC writing	✱	✱	✱	✱	✱	✱	✱	clear progress with source use and integration of evidence

Melanie	topic								notes
FYC 1	abstinence-only education	O	O	O	O	O	O	O	some claims exist in some ¶s; evidence limited to speculation
FYC 2	homeland security	●	●	●	●	●	●	●	employs claims and provides evidence in support
WAC 3	executive leadership	O	O	O	●	O	O	O	when present, claims lack concision, clarity; evidence often flawed

Nikki	topic								notes
FYC 1	rhetorical analysis	O	O	O	O	O	●	O	claims are mostly mere paraphrases, with little support
FYC 2	banning/burning books	●	●	●	●	●	●	✱	awkward, wordy development but purposeful structure
WAC 3	suicide prevalence	●	●	●	●	●	●	●	claims still lack concision; severe limitations in evidence

Rita	topic								notes
FYC 1	minimum wage	○	○	○	○	○	○	○	claims are concise, clear, yet lack development, evidence
FYC 2	gay/lesbian & parenting	○	○	○	○	✻	○	✻	strong source use and integration in support of clear claims
WAC 3	media plan for hotel chain	✻	✻	✻	○	✻	✻	○	very clear, precise claims supported by strong evidence
Sheryl	**topic**								**notes**
FYC 1	rhetorical analysis	○	○	○	○	○	○	○	paragraphs begin with blunt topic sentences, usually paraphrases
FYC 2	autodidactic literacy	✻	○	✻	✻	✻	✻	✻	clear, focused, qualified claims with consistent evidence
WAC 3	uncertainty (oncology/obstetrics)	✻	○	✻	✻	✻	✻	✻	generally clear and qualified claims with strong evidence in support
Steve	**topic**								**notes**
FYC 1	anti-poverty aid	○	○	○	○	○	○	○	clear claims, competent development, no documentation
FYC 2	anti-Americanism	○	○	○	○	○	○	○	little/no progress except for documentation
WAC 3	thermo-mechanical analyzer	○	○	○	○	○	○	○	only some ¶s employ claims, but basic structure is observed

Legend: ○ problematic   ○ acceptable   ✻ exemplary

1. First-Year Composition, Start of Term

At the beginning of first-year composition, students' writing demonstrated a number of difficulties with articulating and supporting claims. The first formal writing task prompted all students to "articulate and support a clear position on an issue raised by the assigned reading," and, in the process of doing so, to "formulate intelligent claims and make purposeful, appropriately documented use of authoritative sources as supporting evidence." Most of the twelve students in this study were able to compose paragraphs with discernible topic sentences, ones that directed the essay from one subtopic to the next, and in fact, with few exceptions, nearly every body paragraph from nearly every student paper began with such a sentence. That paragraphs begin with topic sentences appears to be a convention thoroughly inculcated in these students' prior learning. Yet at this stage, just three students were able to formulate claims and support them with documented evidence.

Nine students struggled to articulate claims that posited arguable, supported propositions separate from the evidence intended to support them. Amy, for instance, argues that "Texas, which accepts more money than any other state for abstinence-only education funds, which is more than 12 million dollars annually, has the fifth-highest teen pregnancy rating"[2]—in the process conflating her claim with the evidence intended to support it. More commonly, students managed to separate claims from the evidence offered in their support, as Claire does here: "When most teenagers turn 16 the first thing on their mind is getting their license and all they care

---

2. All examples of student writing are presented verbatim, with any errors or inelegancies left intact and unmarked.

about is taking their friends out and driving around." The claim lacks concision, and the evidence that follows is lax, but the point is sufficiently clear.

Only on occasion did students articulate claims that were models of concision. In an essay on euphemisms in the debate over vegetarianism, for instance, Mary claims "Supporters of vegetarianism tend to use words that stir the emotions." Often when students were able to articulate claims of fact, value, or policy in an arguable proposition, as Mary does above, they struggled with concision and precision. For instance, this claim of Hailey's could easily—and more effectively—be articulated in significantly fewer words: "Another issue that could arise if the minimum wage were increased would be the number of people dropping out of high school could increase." And at times, difficulties with precision and concision rendered students' claims obtuse, as is the case in this example from Kate: "Two extremes are present among parents involving their influence on their children. Although there is a middle between the extremes, the highest level of influence is present at opposite ends of the scale."

While students at the beginning of FYC exhibited a conceptual understanding of claims as a structural device, though not a developed ability to articulate them with precision and concision, their use of supporting evidence was limited. In a few cases, students struggled to provide any instances of supporting evidence. Claire's claim above about newly-licensed teen drivers, for example, is unsupported by any fact, statistic, testimony, or anecdote. Hailey follows her claim about minimum wage not with supporting evidence but with idle speculation: "If you were able to get a pretty decent paying job without even graduating high school then why would you waste your time at high school when you could be making respectable money somewhere where you didn't need a degree." And Amy, having already confused her claim and her evidence, develops her idea only by explaining her confusion: "If someone could explain those numbers to me, and how it makes sense that so much money doesn't help the gigantic state, the abstinence only education is quite obviously not helping the Texas area, why should it work anywhere else?" These writers' difficulties supporting claims with any specific source-based evidence severely limits their abilities to argue successfully.

More common for these first-year writers, though, was the simple tactic of supporting a claim with one or two simple instances of evidence in support. Melanie, for instance, supports this reasonably concise, unambiguous claim—"More and more people are starting to conclude that the abstinence-only message is ineffective with teens"—with two facts: first, that ten states refuse federal money, and second, that of the remaining 40, Texas receives the greatest amount. Yet neither directly supports the claim as written, and no source is correctly acknowledged. While all of the students whose work we examined demonstrated difficulty with documenting sources, a few of them managed to support their claims with more concrete examples and evidence, even when documentation was missing or incomplete. For instance, Mary's claim about the language of vegetarianism is supported with a quoted appeal to authority: "PETA (People for the Ethical Treatment of Animals) describes many animals as having human characteristics."

In sum, as they started FYC, all twelve students exhibited at least a rudimentary knowledge of paragraph development: all of them employed basic strategies of separating subtopics or reasoning into discrete paragraphs and nearly always began those paragraphs with topic sentences. Often, however, those topic sentences did little more than announce new subtopics; rarely did they posit arguable propositions. When they were able to articulate claims, students at this stage demonstrated a number of difficulties, primarily with precision and concision, but also with presenting the claim as a discrete entity, separate from its supporting evidence. The evidence used in support of claims, meanwhile, when provided, is often self- rather than source-based, frequently insufficient, and sometimes less than fully supportive of the claim it is intended to develop.

2. First-Year Composition, End of Term

Near the conclusion of first-year composition, the students wrote a second paper in response to the same prompt that had motivated their earlier papers. As before, all twelve demonstrated command of topic sentences and the basics of paragraphing. After a semester of instruction, all twelve also had made progress with regard to formulating claims. However, there were considerable differences in the amount of improvement students demonstrated.

Four of the students (Lois, Kate, Mary, and Sheryl) consistently formulated claims that were both arguable and also supportable with documented evidence. In a paper on the benefits of bilingual education, Mary's claims in particular stand out for their concision and appropriateness: "Second, bilingual education allows students to retain their own cultural identity while learning another language." More usual among these four, though, are claims that are clear and arguable but lacking in concision, like this one from Lois's paper aimed at debunking various 9/11 conspiracies: "Since the three attacks on the Pentagon and the World Trade Center, and adding the attempted attack proposed by Flight 93 on the Capital building, almost every single official finding, piece of evidence, or fact presented to support the government's research has been brought under suspicion and scrutiny."

The remaining eight students also improved their ability to articulate claims that were supportable with documented evidence, though unlike the four students discussed above, their efforts were more often problematic. Some claims, for instance, were overly simplistic, as Nikki's is in her argument against censorship: "The ability to read is a very useful and powerful quality that a large number of people have the capability of doing." Melanie posits a similarly oversimplified claim in her paper on homeland security: "One of the biggest changes after 9/11 was the enforcement of the USA Patriot Act." Though they are perhaps arguable, simplistic claims like these simply do not prepare the way for these writers to advance a delineated line of supporting evidence. Among the remaining eight students, there are also occasional examples of claims that are more expansive than can be treated well in the single paragraph. In his paper about the roots of anti-Americanism, Steve offers a grammatically suspect example: "Anti-Americanism is not a new idea; it has been around for decades; somewhat derived from America's beliefs and concepts of how the world should be run." While these examples indicate that not all twelve students had learned to formulate arguable claims with perfect consistency, this salient point remains: by the conclusion of FYC, all twelve students were regularly attempting to make claims that were supportable with documented evidence, even if at times their claims were in need of improvement.

One area where improvement was especially recognizable was in students' ability to qualify the claims they were making. At the start of first-year composition, nine of the twelve students had made no effort to qualify claims. However, at the conclusion of the course only two, Claire and Evan, still offered no instances of qualification. For Evan, this appears to be because he was still struggling to keep his claims and the ensuing argument separate from one another, as shown here in his paper on the effects of the Patriot Act: "The Patriot Act is a violation of American citizen's rights. It crosses the line between protecting Americans and invading privacy. Is it worth giving up our rights to feel a little bit safer?" The remaining ten students were at least occasionally able to qualify their claims, though qualification was not necessarily a consistent feature of their work. For example, in her paper arguing in support of the parental rights of gay and lesbian parents, Rita occasionally presents claims devoid of the sort of qualifiers that would help to focus her argument: "gays should be able to adopt children because being good parents has to do with their ability to love and support children, not with their sexual orientation." Later in the same paper, however, she qualifies some of her claims effectively: "There are *some* opponents of gay rights who argue that..." (emphasis added). For two students, Kate and Sheryl, qualification of claims had clearly become a regular feature of academic argumentation, as demonstrated in a claim Sheryl makes in a paper about autodidactic literacy: "Many governments wish to restrict their citizens to a narrow group of ideas and realize that people are more willing to conform if they do not have the power of books; therefore, people in these societies that choose to read face problems using the knowledge they gain." Demonstrating the writers' understanding of the value of qualifying terms (e.g., *many, few, some,* etc.), both Kate's and Sheryl's end-of-term papers qualify claims consistently.

At the end of FYC, students were still learning to marshal appropriate evidence to support their claims. As they had at the start of the course, some students were still struggling to provide sound supporting evidence. Hailey's claim about illegal immigrants taking jobs from American citizens, for instance, offers no real support other than undocumented anecdotal evidence: "a dry wall business owner said…." Steve attempts to support his claim about the source of anti-Americanism with a loose discussion of Cold War history, moving improbably from the Cuban Missile Crisis forward all the way to the Iraq War, a discussion he manages with little documentation or concrete evidence. And Lois tries to debunk a range of 9/11 conspiracy theories using little more than her own developing powers of reason. These three problematic examples notwithstanding, eleven of the twelve students did make progress in supporting their claims with appropriate documented evidence.

Students developed increasingly sophisticated means of supporting their arguments. Recall that at the start of the course Rita was unsure how to support her argument about minimum wage: "most of these people who earn the minimum are young people looking for pocket money, not poor families; therefore, the main purpose of the raise, reduce poverty, won't be achieved." However, in her paper arguing against discrimination towards gay and lesbian parents at the end of FYC, she demonstrates a keen ability to construct a source-based argument. In a paragraph opening with the qualified claim that "Many studies have proven this belief wrong after comparing children raised by gay and heterosexual parents," Rita weaves in four separate citations, each one introduced in accurate APA format with signal phrases that establish the credentials of the experts she quotes or paraphrases. Claire, a student who began FYC relying on her own opinions to support her argument about newly licensed teen drivers, at the end of the course supports her argument against school uniforms with appeals to authority ("Ackerman states in 'White Tops, Grey Bottoms' that…") and quotations from students she interviewed for the paper. While none of the twelve had completely mastered the use of appropriate evidence in support of their claims, all had moved away from the self-focused evidence that was a common feature of their writing at the start of the course. Mary's paper in support of bilingual education is a representative example of the gains students tended to make as they learned to use documented evidence: her paper cites and uses appropriately five sources.

As they concluded FYC, then, all twelve students had improved on the knowledge of paragraph development they possessed at the start of the course. Additionally, all twelve had made some progress with regard to articulation of appropriate claims, though there are examples in their work of claims in need of greater concision, qualification, and complexity. Of the twelve students, eleven demonstrated improvement in their ability to use documented evidence in support of their claims, having moved beyond the self-focused argumentation that characterized their initial papers for the course. Even for the one student (Evan) whose improvement was slight, there was progress in formulating claims, concision, and documentation. Over the course of FYC, then, all but one of the students markedly improved their ability to construct source-based academic arguments.

3. Writing Across the Curriculum

As upper-division students writing across the curriculum and in various majors, students demonstrated a range of capabilities with regard to articulating and supporting claims. For seven of the twelve students (Claire, Hailey, Kate, Lois, Mary, Rita, and Sheryl), progress begun in FYC continued throughout the undergraduate degree, resulting in academic writing often (or in four students' cases, always) characterized by clear, qualified, and concise claims supported by appropriate documented evidence. For three of the remaining students (Evan, Nikki and Steve), development appears to have stagnated as they transitioned into writing in the major fields of study. These students at times demonstrated competence in the assessed areas, though, in places, issues that were problematic in FYC remained troublesome three years later. And, in two cases (Amy and Melanie), students seem to have regressed as writers, their senior-level work evidencing problems that were not present in their work at the end of FYC. These two cases aside, the general picture that emerges across the group is one of competence gained, particularly when compared to their writing as incoming students.

Ten of the twelve students were either always or nearly always able to articulate supportable claims in the papers we examined. However, the variation of students' majors dictated a considerable range in the types of claims students made. For example, in a course for her nursing major, Hailey's claims concern care procedures, as illustrated by this sentence from a paper on preeclampsia prevention: "Even though there is not a cure for preeclampsia there are things that the nurse can do to aid in the prevention of complications." Similarly, as a major in mechanical engineering, in his lab reports Steve now formulates claims related to correct experimental procedures: "Before anything can be inserted into the [Thermo-Mechanical Analyzer], the samples must be correctly prepared." For Hailey (Nursing) and Steve (Mechanical Engineering) as well as Kate (Biology), Rita (Advertising), and Sheryl (Nursing), the fundamental purpose of claims is not quite the same as it had been in first-year composition. Specifically, rather than setting up source-based argumentation, for each of these five writers claims now create rhetorical space for explaining results of an experiment (Kate, Steve), describing specific procedures (Hailey, Kate, Rita, Sheryl, Steve) or advocating for a precise course of action (Hailey, Rita, Sheryl).

The remaining seven students were in disciplines that required claims that were more closely aligned rhetorically with those they had made in FYC. Some articulated concise claims supportable by documented evidence with consistency, as illustrated by this example from Lois's (Psychology) library-based research paper on eating disorders: "A new policy called *I Like Me* should be created to help teens deal with and prevent eating disorders." Lois draws on academic journal articles for support, introducing each source with a clear, effective signal phrase and formatting her in-text citations in accurate APA style. Slightly more complicated are some of Mary's (TESOL/Spanish Education) claims, as demonstrated in this sentence from an empirical study she conducted on second language learners' ability to retrieve memories stored in their first language: "Researchers believe that if more information can be gathered about how information storage and retrieval occurs, we will better understand the mental processes of first- and second-language writers." Mary supports her claim with evidence from three separate studies, each cited accurately in APA format. In these papers both Lois and Mary demonstrate consistently their sharpened understandings of the way to formulate and support claims in their respective disciplines.

Other students struggled to articulate workable claims consistently. For instance, in a research paper on juvenile justice, Claire (Pre-Law) conflates two claims with one another: "It is a known fact that the effect of a treatment program varies depending on the individual offender. Treatment programs are designed to change the life course of young offenders and deter them from getting involved with juvenile justice." While her work sometimes provides successful claims, Nikki (Health Promotion) on occasion struggles with clarity, as in this example from a research paper on suicide prevalence: "This issue of being in a rural area is a large factor of difficult access to healthcare." Nikki does show some ability to formulate appropriate claims, though her support often takes the form of loose, awkward paraphrasing of source articles. Consider, for example, this excerpt from an essay on the prevalence of suicide in urban vs. rural areas: "A research article that was addressed is by Gessert (2003), it suggests that rurality may serve as a marker for low levels of social combination and that social and demographic change may have affected rural areas more undesirability [sic] than urban areas." Nikki does not address the source subsequently in her essay, missing the opportunity to articulate more precisely how the article advances a connected line of reasoning. Nikki repeats this pattern throughout the paper, resulting in an essay that consists of a sequential presentation of source summaries.

Though at times some claims are problematic, only two students did not demonstrate the ability to formulate claims supportable by documented evidence. As he had in FYC, Evan (Pre-Law) still struggles to separate his claims and evidence from one another, as in this passage from a historical research essay on the insanity defense: "The case of Charles Guiteau is a good example of why the McNaughton Rule was insufficient. Guiteau was obviously insane, but was found guilty when he should have been found not guilty by reason of insanity." Although Evan follows this with one and half pages detailing the Guiteau case, the text reads more like an encyclopedia entry about his subject rather than as an argument for how Guiteau's conviction exemplifies the insufficiency of the McNaughton Rule. Similarly, Melanie (Business Education) struggles to articulate sound claims, a surprising finding given that she had made progress in this area during first-year composition. As a senior, however, her claims lack both precision and direction, as evidenced in this example from a paper on the role of executive leadership in contemporary business: "Looking at four different studies they imply that leadership does not effect an organization, but once correcting some methodological problems with the studies they actually show a much larger impact that leadership does make." From here, Melanie offers four quick bullet points paraphrasing the four studies she refers to, but she does not articulate or address any of the "methodological problems" referred to in her claim.

At the conclusion of FYC, most of these students were still learning to support their claims with appropriate evidence. Over the course of their undergraduate degrees, however, six of them (Kate, Lois, Mary, Rita, Sheryl, and to a slightly lesser extent Hailey) had clearly improved upon the gains they made in FYC, reaching a point where claims were regularly supported with carefully selected and arranged evidence. Three of the students (Claire, Nikki, Steve), showed the ability to articulate claims, even if at times they struggled to produce writing where all claims were formulated appropriately and supported sufficiently. The remaining three students (Amy, Evan, Melanie) all struggled to formulate appropriate claims, producing instead either writing that conflated claims and evidence (Evan) or that was confused in its use of evidence and support (Amy, Melanie). As indicated by their writing in FYC, students generally began their university careers with little ability to formulate and support their claims in writing; however, as upper-division students writing across the curriculum, nine of the twelve made clear progress, expanding on and adapting improvements begun in FYC to meet the increasingly specific needs of their chosen fields of study.

Discussion

If one goal of first-year composition is to foster students' ability to articulate claims and present compelling evidence in support—as is very much the case at these students' institution—the evidence from this study suggests that the majority of students improved these abilities. All twelve of the students in the study demonstrated at least a degree of improvement in at least one area; ten of the twelve made gains in multiple areas.

In some cases, the record of students' improvement was quite impressive, as evidenced in selected WAC papers from students' final year of undergraduate study. Consider, for instance, the six students whose uses of claims and evidence was in at least some respects exemplary in their WAC courses; all six had evidenced "problematic" work in more than one area at the start of FYC. For these writers, a path of improvement begun in FYC appears to have continued throughout the course and into WAC. Six of these students—Kate, Lois, Mary, Rita, Claire, Sheryl—demonstrate consistent development in nearly every respect and have become, near the conclusion of their college careers, adept at articulating challenging, concise, and qualified claims supported with researched evidence from a variety of authoritative sources. A seventh student, Hailey, had at least learned to use claims and evidence with consistency, if not great success.

For three others, evidence of improvement was less clear. Competent but not consistent, Steve, for example, is at the end of his studies little changed from the writer he was when he began work at the university. Similarly, Nikki's work as a senior is much as it had been at the conclusion of FYC, though it bears mentioning that she did chart improvement in multiple areas as an incoming freshman. Evan shows improvement in some of the areas, though in others his work remains conspicuously unchanged.

Two of the students, Melanie and Amy, did not make substantive improvements past FYC and, in some ways, showed signs of regression from their first year. Of course, as Smit (2004) contends, transfer is unpredictable and variable, a reminder that student writing ability is hardly static. Quite likely some of the students in this study who struggled may well experience success in other rhetorical contexts; by extension, the students who demonstrated competence may encounter rhetorical contexts that prove difficult to navigate. While our research methodology precludes final judgments on any of the writers participating in this study, the larger picture emerging from this research suggests that most students improved their ability to compose increasingly challenging academic arguments over the course of their undergraduate degrees.

Generic Variety, Rhetorical Constancy

Even our small sample size demonstrates the considerable variety of tasks student writers face across the curriculum. For the purposes of comparison, Table 1 lists the genres participants were asked to produce in their major fields of study. It should be noted here that we did not solicit an exhaustive list of all of the projects students completed across the curriculum; indeed, such a list, were it even possible to create with accuracy, would be extremely long. Rather, our participants volunteered a list of the projects they had worked on recently. For some students, the variety of genres far exceeds even that indicated. Mary, for instance, seeking a dual teaching degree (with coursework in Spanish, TESOL, and Education) while taking additional courses in English Literature and Chinese, as well as multiple internships and independent studies, had undertaken a vast array of writing experiences, from workplace tasks to blogs to reviews and other analytical papers in addition to the tasks listed above.

Yet despite this variety, all twelve of the students engaged in writing tasks that required them to articulate claims and support them with evidence. Even though our participants' majors spread across a range of disciplinary areas—liberal arts, physical sciences, social sciences, engineering, education, nursing—the rhetorical constancy of the need to support ideas with evidence suggests that the students' training in FYC was relevant to their future writing tasks. Indeed, while audiences, formats, lengths, topics, and conventions all varied from task to task, one frequent constant was that these students were often expected—sometimes explicitly, sometimes more implicitly—to structure their prose so as to support claims with evidence. While all students in the study brought to their FYC course a rudimentary understanding of topic sentences and paragraph development, this knowledge was clearly less than sufficient for advanced writing across the curriculum. Instead, each of them had to develop and improve their abilities to articulate and support claims, even as they faced increasingly varied and sophisticated tasks.

Skills Transfer: From First-Year Composition to Writing Across the Curriculum

While the students in this study encountered in WAC a diverse variety of genres, most of those genres required them to support claims with evidence. In this regard, students appeared to benefit from related instruction in FYC. That is to say, students' development of ability to articulate and support claims in FYC appeared directly related to their ability to do so in their later WAC courses. All twelve participants developed their abilities to articulate and support claims while in FYC, and all of them were expected to employ those abilities in their WAC courses. Nine of the twelve were able to continue that improvement, but perhaps the more salient point is the relevance of FYC to WAC. Even though many FYC students do not have declared majors and fewer still can predict what writing tasks await them in the future, for all of the students in this study, the instruction and practice in composing claims and presenting evidence proved to be of value. As evidenced in their actual prose, most students benefited from that instruction during FYC and many continued to adapt that knowledge to their WAC as they undertook and completed their majors.

Given its relevance to these students' later experience in WAC courses, dedicated practice in articulating and supporting claims appears to be a vital part of their FYC instruction. For FYC instructors and program administrators, this kind of direct instruction will likely be relevant to students' future work in a number of majors.

Eventually students will need to learn far more than methods of articulating and supporting claims, and they may well go on to work in a variety of genres. However, helping to develop students' articulation, concision, and qualification of claims, and instructing them directly in finding and presenting different kinds of evidence from researched sources, is work that can have a direct impact on students' later writing across the curriculum, even when any given student may go on to any of a number of possible majors.

For those who teach in or direct WAC programs, to us it would seem that continued attention to students' claims and evidence while in the upper division is advisable. If students have encountered such instruction in FYC, discussion of claims and evidence in WAC will relate directly to meaningful foundational work, an idea that reinforces Greene and Orr's (2007) work on transfer from FYC to WAC within the first year of students' university careers. Even as college juniors and seniors, student writers can benefit from direct instruction in the practice of composing claims. Tasks that require them to support claims with evidence can promote their understanding if the assignment directions and evaluation criteria emphasize these features. And instructors' feedback, whether offered on work-in-progress or the final product (or both), can attend to such matters as concision, qualification, and support.

The participants in this study all were routinely expected to compose in ways that required advanced uses of claims and evidence in their upper-division courses. Those who succeeded in doing so succeeded more generally at their writing tasks, just as those who struggled to articulate and support claims struggled more generally as well. For those who succeed as well as those who struggle, any opportunity for direct instruction, guided practice, and/or individualized feedback aimed at improving this vital skill is likely to relate not only to the task at hand but to the writer's prior experience, and to his or her continued development in the future. Ideally, the undergraduate experience, from first-year composition to writing across the curriculum, should provide contexts, opportunities, and feedback to foster that development.

REFERENCES

Beaufort, A. (2007). *College writing and beyond: A new framework for university writing instruction*. Logan, UT: Utah State University Press.

Carroll, L. A. (2002). *Rehearsing new roles: How college students develop as writers*. Carbondale, IL: Southern Illinois University Press.

Dias, P., Freedman, A., Medway, P., & Paré, A. (1999). *Worlds apart: Acting and writing in academic and workplace contexts*. Mahwah, NJ: Erlbaum.

Fukuzawa, S., & Boyd, C. (2008). The writing development initiative: A pilot project to help students become proficient writers. *CELT, 1*, 123-26.

Graff, G. (2003). *Clueless in academe: How schooling obscures the life of the mind*. New Haven, CT: Yale University Press.

Greene, S., & Orr, A. J. (2007). First-year college students writing across the disciplines. In P. O'Neill (Ed.), *Blurring boundaries: Developing writers, researchers and teachers: A tribute to William L. Smith* (pp. 123-56). Cresskill, NJ: Hampton.

Herrington, A. (1985). Writing in academic settings: A study of the contexts for writing in two college chemical engineering courses. *Research in the Teaching of English, 19*(3), 331-59.

Herrington, A., & Curtis, M. (2000). *Persons in process: Four stories of writing and personal development in college*. Urbana, IL: NCTE.

Hillocks, G., Jr. (2010). Teaching argument for critical thinking and writing: An introduction. *English Journal, 99*(6), 24-32.

Hillocks, G., Jr. (2011). *Teaching argument writing: Supporting claims with relevant evidence and clear reasoning*. Portsmouth, NH: Heinemann.

McCarthy, L. P. (1987). A stranger in strange lands: A college student writing across the curriculum. *Research in the Teaching of English, 21*, 233-65.

Rose, M. (1989). *Lives on the boundary*. New York, NY: Penguin.

Smit, D. W. (2004). *The end of composition studies*. Carbondale, IL: Southern Illinois University Press.

Thaiss, C., & Zawacki, T. M. (2006). *Engaged writers and dynamic disciplines: Research on the academic writing life*. Portsmouth, NH: Boynton/Cook.

Toulmin, S. E. (2003). *The uses of argument* (Updated ed.). New York, NY: Cambridge University Press (Original work published 1958).

Walvoord, B. E., & McCarthy, L. P. (1990). *Thinking and writing in college: A naturalistic study of students in four disciplines*. Urbana, IL: NCTE.

Wardle, E. (2007). Understanding "transfer" from FYC: Preliminary results of a longitudinal study. *WPA: Writing Program Administration, 31*(1-2), 65-85.

From High School to College: Developing Writing Skills in the Disciplines

VIRGINIA CRANK

ALL COLLEGE TEACHERS across the curriculum face a challenge when helping first-year students develop college-level writing skills. The gap between high school and college writing can complicate interactions between students, who often believe that their high school English teachers (particularly in college-prep courses) have given them all the tools they need for success in writing at college, and college teachers, who have only a vague idea of what this high school writing instruction looks like. It would be useful for all college teachers to know what their incoming students know and understand about writing in order to fix this disconnect. A review of research on the transition from high school to college writing reveals a set of six key terms or concepts (genre/format, sources, argument, process, audience, and voice) that are commonly used in both high school and college writing classes. Knowing how teachers and students have used these terms in high school can help college teachers connect with their students in such a way as to build on the writing skills they bring with them. Teachers in every discipline, either purposefully or indirectly, teach their students what it means to write in college and can benefit from an examination of, in particular, three of these concepts: genre/format, argument, and authority/voice. Using these three to talk with their students about the discourse community of their discipline, college teachers across the disciplines can offer students a greater sense of building upon the writing they did in high school.

Tiane Donahue's 2007 article in *The Writing Instructor* says, "College faculty seem to know little about what high school teachers are asking students to do and why, and less about what high school students bring with them to the college writing classroom." The lack of knowledge suggested by Donahue's article becomes almost prohibitive when college instructors discuss the difficulty of teaching students who seem overwhelmed by and unprepared for the writing and reading tasks assigned to them. This frustration has spawned at least two collections of essays in the past six years: *What is College-Level Writing? Vols. 1 and 2*. These two volumes and a flurry of scholarly activity on the relationship between high school and college writing in just the last two years—Addison and McGee (2010); Applebee and Langer (2009 and 2011); Sullivan, Tinberg and Blau (2010); Hansen and Farris (2010); Taczak and Thelin (2009); Tinberg and Nadeau (June 2011)—have all brought to our attention the "space between" high school and college writing. Some of this conversation has been about the lack of writing in secondary schools; some has been about the increasing popularity of dual-enrollment programs. These are fruitful discussions that will have significant impact at the programmatic level in teaching writing at the secondary and post-secondary level as well as in preparing writing teachers. What I seek to do in this synthesis of the research is to pull out certain threads of discussion that might help college teachers who use WAC/WID methodologies better assist students in making the transition to college-level writing. I'll begin by briefly discussing what recent research shows to be the limitations of high school writing practices, touching on the so-called "deficits" of incoming freshmen. The bulk of the essay will then describe how the body of research into the transition between high school and college writing reveals three key terms/concepts relevant to transitioning into writing across the curriculum. The essay ends with a call to resist the widespread belief that writing is a set of low-level skills that can be learned once and be "out of the way."

Constraints in High School English

In reviewing the literature (which includes more than eighty articles, books, and dissertations over the last sixty years), there seems to be a clear consensus among writing teachers and researchers—in comments quantitative, qualitative, and purely anecdotal—that students entering college are not fully prepared to do the kinds of writing tasks required of them at college. Recent data from Sharlene Kiuhara, Steve Graham, and Leanne Hawken, in a 2009 article in the *Journal of Educational Psychology*, shows that "Collectively, almost one half of the [secondary] teachers across the three disciplines [language arts, sciences, and social studies] (47%) did not assign at least one ... multiparagraph activity at least monthly. On a weekly basis, 80% of teachers did not assign at least one of these activities. When such activities were assigned, teachers were most likely to ask students to write a five-paragraph theme or a persuasive essay" (143). They also indicated that "a sizable proportion of the participating teachers seldom assigned activities that clearly involved writing multiple paragraphs. Almost one third of language arts and social studies teachers did not assign such an activity monthly" (151).

Additionally, Arthur Applebee and Judith Langer's most recent report of their research into writing instruction in middle and high schools (2011) shows that even though students in middle and high school are writing more than they did thirty years ago, only 12.3% of the time in English classes "was devoted to writing of at least a paragraph length" and "only 19% [of the 8542 assignments they analyzed] represented extended writing of a paragraph or more; the rest consisted of fill in the blank and short answer exercises, and copying of information directly from teacher's presentation—types of activities that are best described as writing without composing" (15). High school teachers, they say, report that only 41.1% of the total grade for English would be based on writing of at least a paragraph length: "writing on average matters less than multiple choice or short answer questions in assessing performance in English" (18).

The results of several other large-scale empirical studies, all of which offer a similar picture, are delineated in a 2010 *College Composition and Communication* article by Joann Addison and Sharon McGee. The body of research says again and again that even though secondary English teachers are clearly more engaged in process-oriented writing instruction, students still do not write enough in high school, that they do not write for specific audiences and purposes, that they do not write in multiple genres, that they are bound by formulas and rules, and that they primarily write responses to literature. The Common Core State Standards for K-12 Language Arts instruction, developed by the National Governors Association for Best Practices and now adopted by 45 states, may change things, as the standards call for more writing in all classes and in response to more nonfiction texts. We may see that as students write more in all disciplines and on more nonfiction texts that they are coming to college with a more sophisticated approach to understanding how writers make choices and decisions based on rhetorical contexts.

At present, however, the research in the field confirms our experiential understanding that students will experience writing very differently in college than they did in high school and explores how these differences complicate the transition from writing in high school to writing in college. Susan Fanetti, Kathy Bushrow and David DeWeese categorize the differences this way: "High school education is designed to be standardized and quantifiable. College education is designed to be theoretical" (77-78). They assert, "High school students learn to follow a specific set of rules; college students learn that there are no rules—or, better, that the rules change daily" (78). While this delineation is somewhat oversimplified, given the nature of some testing and assessment protocols related to college writing, it does reflect a general shift in thinking about composition that will challenge students when they enter college.

It would be difficult for those of us who teach and have always taught at the college level to truly understand the power and influence of the external pressures that lead secondary teachers away from using writing more often as a tool for either instruction or assessment. The best-intentioned, most rhetorically-driven secondary teachers see themselves time and again brought up short in their ambitions by schooling systems (local, regional, and national) that are constantly shifting and recalculating the ways they measure student success. These shifts are driven by political, economic, and social forces that truly overwhelm the individual teacher in her classroom. Applebee and Langer report that teachers feel obligated to prepare students for high-stakes testing situations, and that those tests are having "a very direct and limiting effect on classroom emphases" (18); they note that "55.1% of English teachers reported frequent practices in timed, on-demand writing" (19), concluding that, "Given the constraints imposed by high-stakes tests, writing as a way to study, learn, and go beyond—as a way to construct knowledge or generate new networks of understandings—is rare" (26). This is, again, not to say that innovation and evidence-based writing instruction never happen, but when they do, it is sometimes against incredible odds.

Key Concepts/Terms for Understanding the Transition

A college teacher can expect, given the data reported, that her students will have had far less experience in and exposure to the kinds of writing practices she will want to incorporate in her classes. Where does the WAC/WID-focused teacher begin to bridge the gap between what her students know/can do and what she will ask them to do? The key to helping new students make the transition to writing in the disciplines may be a small set of terms or concepts that teachers on both sides of the transition use, terms that often have different implications, meanings or associated practices in each of the cultures. If first-year college instructors in every discipline can understand how these terms or concepts are used in high school writing/English classes, we can offer definitions, explanations, and activities to our students that will build that bridge.

Genre/format, argument, and authority/voice—the terms analyzed in this essay—come directly from reading the available research on the transition to college writing. These concepts emerged repeatedly in discussions of what students do in high school writing, what they do in college writing, what teachers emphasize at each level, and what skills writers need to succeed in writing at the college level. Certainly we see the terms coming up in discussions of writing at each level, but how they are used—their definition, practice, and reinforcement—illustrates the differences in culture that lead researchers to characterize high school as standardized and college as theoretical (see reference above to Fannetti, Bushrow, and DeWeese).

This characterization, unfortunately, seems to cast both high school and college as homogenous and monolithic cultures—a tendency well debunked by Victoria Cobb in her 2002 dissertation, "From Where They Sit: Stories of Students Making the Transition from High School Writing to College Writing." Cobb rejects the term *culture* for describing high school as creating a false sense of homogeneity, preferring to analyze the discourse communities (or "Discourses") students experience in high school and college (2-4). Cobb's critique of the tendency to see high school as a homogenous culture can also be applied to discussions of college or "college-level writing." Most research and scholarship about the transition from high school to college writing assumes that first-year college students will be entering writing classrooms that share some similarities of approach, pedagogy, theoretical underpinning, or purpose when this is in fact inaccurate and optimistic. If our secondary colleagues are constrained by external forces that demand they teach and evaluate in certain ways, our post-secondary colleagues in English (or the department that oversees first-year writing requirements) sometimes suffer from having absolutely no constraints on what and how they teach in first-year writing classes. So, Fanetti, Bushrow, and DeWeese may be describing a golden ideal of college-level writing. But in the general view, teachers at the college level teach writing in the context of a specific disciplinary approach to knowledge-making and communicating within a specific discourse community. The difference in how these two educational environments tend to use these three terms/concepts seems connected to how writing practices in college are more likely to grow out of a larger concern for rhetorical awareness and the kinds of discipline and community-based writing skills writers will need as professionals and college graduates rather than as future college students. The higher-education concern with genres, arguments, and voice comes from an understanding of the disciplinary demands of writing—the community demands of writing—whereas the way the terms are used in high school seem stripped of that community-driven context, that understanding of these terms as rhetorical.

The three terms this article will explore are a subset of the useful terms readers can glean from the literature; these three will offer the WAC/WID teacher in particular a way to use terms their students will have heard in high school (English, mostly) as a means of introducing the discipline-specific discourse practices and values they teach. These three terms reveal certain long-held beliefs about the nature and purpose of academic writing and its grounding in critical thinking and community-based reasoning; they are common language we share for talking about how writers first learn and then join any discourse community.

Genre/Format

Easily the most discussed "problem" that first-year college writers face is their lack of understanding of genre/format. Many articles and books argue that student writers are constrained by their limited understanding of how content affects format, and their consequent reliance on a limited range of formats and genres for writing. Kathleen Blake Yancey reports on research conducted at the University of Washington and the University of Tennessee that confirms that "students brought a limited genre knowledge into college with them and didn't use that knowledge when writing" (304).

The research by Kiuhara, Graham, and Hawken offers some specific ideas about the genres incoming college writers will have practiced:

> The most common writing activities used by teachers were short answer responses to homework, responses to material read, completing worksheets, and summary of materials read. . . . The next most common writing activities were journal entries and lists. . . . This was followed by writing step-by-step instructions and five-paragraph essays. (140)

Their research shows us that entering college freshmen will likely have had some experience with five-paragraph essays, reading responses, and journals; about half will have had some experience with research papers; very few will have ever been assigned to write e-mails, memos, and business letters.

David Smit identifies this limited understanding of genre conventions as the most serious difference between high school and college writing and as a serious flaw in writing instruction at all levels. He asserts, "a great deal, if not most, of what passes for writing instruction at the secondary and college levels in this country is rule-ridden and formulaic and unrelated to writing as it is actually done by people who write" (73). He believes that a lack of attention to the social contexts of writing leads to an ignorance of genre and that "writing teachers [are] providing little useful information about how various genres are actually written; I see a great deal of instruction in how to write using rules, formats, and formulas and little practice in actually writing" (73). Smit's observations confirm the experiences of most of us who teach or use any kind of writing in college.

At this point, it would be useful to talk about the difference between the rules and formulas so denigrated by Smit (and others) and genre conventions. Why are "rules" bad and "conventions" good? The answer lies in teaching students that writing is always a response to particular rhetorical situations and within discourse communities. Scholars like Smit see "rules" as de-contextualized directives for writing judged as good or bad based on criteria not shared or created by a group of language users; the judgments are often arbitrary or idiosyncratic, or even contradictory. Rules or formulas are usually de-contextualized or contextualized only in solipsistic school settings: "we write like this in high school because you'll be expected to write like this in college." The resulting texts often represent school-bound genres that bear little resemblance to authentic texts read or written outside of the classroom. In contrast, genre conventions are always social, the results of ongoing negotiations of groups of readers and writers who share a common set of values and uses for discourse; as such, the conventions are obeyed because of a desire to reach a real audience and/or participate in a conversation about something of interest to the community.

Christine Farris's essay "Minding the Gap" offers some explanation for the limited instruction in genre in both high school and college. She says that although high school and college teachers are both interested in "developing students' critical understanding," more high school teachers than ever feel the pressure to teach "accessible formats for writing-on-demand" (273). Peter Kittle and Rochelle Ramay agree, saying that one particular genre of academic writing—"the formal-register essay"—has monopolized writing in secondary school: "The emphasis on accountability in the No Child Left Behind Act has resulted in an increased prominence of standardized written forms in the public school sphere—a prominence that does not lend itself to effective college writing. Formulaic writing . . . ends up becoming the de facto genre for academic expression in too many educational settings" (100-101). Teachers, then, are not sacrificing genre flexibility in their writers so much as they are responding to the demands of "stakeholders" who use de-contextualized formulas for writing in order to measure something other than rhetorical fluency.

The specific recipient of this criticism is the five-paragraph theme. Indeed, college composition instructors in particular can expect that most of their students will know and like the five-paragraph essay format. The research by Kiuhara, Graham, and Hawken showed that 83% of Language Arts teachers have students write five-paragraph themes with the frequency of once-a-quarter to daily. Only 7% said they never have students write five-paragraph themes. Joseph Jones's survey of high school students reinforces this frequency; when 300 seniors at a fairly elite high school in Tuscon, Arizona, were asked, Which types of writing have been most emphasized in your high school courses over the past two years? the most common responses, in order, were "the five paragraph essay" and "research reports."

Reliance on this formula serves high school writing instruction in at least one important capacity—test preparation—but it is also most likely true that some secondary English teachers have a limited understanding of how to teach other formats/ genres. Peter Kittle, in describing his experiences as a high school English teacher, admits that he propagated the myth of the five-paragraph essay. "While I readily enough taught this form of writing, I honestly cannot say I looked forward to reading the student work with any relish. But I told my students, as well as myself, that this writing form would serve them well in college" (137). He says that although he believes that correctness and form are both important, that is not why he taught the five-paragraph theme; he taught it out of expedience and an ignorance of what else to teach: "The fact was that I had only vague ideas about what was expected of students when they had to perform at college level, and even less-firm ideas of how to teach students to reach that level" (138). Kittle is probably not in the minority; secondary teachers in general have historically received very little training in teaching writing. Robert Tremmel claims, "It is not uncommon for prospective and beginning teachers—despite their best intentions and the best intentions of their professors—to go through an entire field experience sequence without ever becoming fully involved in the teaching of writing and without ever thinking of themselves as writing teachers" (9). Without direct training in writing instruction, beginning secondary teachers have little background for resisting or working around the external pressures surrounding writing practices.

This lack of training in writing pedagogy may be seen often in college-level instruction as well, both in English departments and in other disciplines, where only certain members of the department are invested in using writing as a way of teaching and using the idea of discourse community as a tool for knowing a discipline. But even amongst those teachers who have not been trained in writing instruction or do not address it specifically in their classes, there is usually an expectation that students will have a more sophisticated understanding of the various genres used in academia than just the five-paragraph theme. In many cases, the teacher expects that students already have a sense of what it means to write in/for their discipline and/or they expect that students will know how to adapt the formulaic writing of high school to the more specifically situated writing of their course.

For a multitude of reasons, college students probably leave high school with a very limited understanding of genre and how it is a part of rhetorically situated writing, preferring instead to rely on formulas designed to teach habits of mind more than actually serve audiences. As these writers enter new discipline-specific discourse communities, college teachers should develop in students (and in themselves) the habit of considering form/genre as entirely dependent on the rhetorical situation and the capacity to think about their writing in the context of the discipline. College teachers, then, should be prepared to explain to the writers in their discipline that formats must be determined by writers, and a class discussion of the uses and limitations of the five-paragraph formula might even help students see both what they can take from it and how they can begin to let it go.

Argument

We move now from the range of possible textual modes contained within the idea of genre/format to the overarching purpose of most texts in any academic discipline: argument. Even in its most detached manifestation, argument—the presentation and support of a position or perspective—has long been seen as the cornerstone of academic writing and is a skill usually heavily emphasized by college teachers. The 2009 NSSE data suggests 80% of college freshmen indicated that most or all of their writing assignments required them to "argue a position using evidence and reasoning" (Addison and McGee 154). While some composition scholars would argue that analysis is the more important skill to teach, as a precursor to argument, *analysis* is not a term used extensively in secondary education, except in connection with the analysis of imaginative or creative literature. Therefore, the term that truly overlaps from high school to college writing is not analysis, but argument.

Gerald Graff and Cathy Birkenstein-Graff go so far as to contend that argument is a "rhetorical fundamental" that can bridge the gap between high school and college writing. They define argument in Burkean terms as "the art of entering a conversation, of summarizing the views of others in order to set up one's own views" and contend that "it is central to every academic department and discipline, from history to microbiology, where practitioners are required to state their views not in isolation, but as a response to what others in the field are saying" (W410).

This definition of argument is, I think, well accepted at the college level. Michael Bernard-Donals describes the process of argument as:

> widening the intellectual context in which arguments are made, and that means giving writers an opportunity to explore not just the "opinions" and "facts" of the case, but also where "opinion" and "fact" bleed into one another depending on which party in the argument you're listening to. Making an argument means not just laying out what you know about an issue (going to the library, mining your own experience), but also finding out what your interlocutor knows and figuring out what common ground you share, what assumptions bind you together, and how opinion and received facts are shaped (and not just "found"). (Alsup and Bernard-Donals 120)

In his description of what argument is at the college level, he also describes how entering students have probably experienced argument in high school: as stating with certainty what you believe to be true, backed up by what you have found. Research by Ron Lunsford, John Kiser, and Deborah Coxwell-Teague confirms this difference in the concept of argument; the authors say that they

> have long noted that the kinds of argumentative writing taught in high school AP courses differs from the argument taught in many college writing courses . . . . the argument essays on the AP exam have been consistently of the thesis and support variety. That is, students may be asked to write about argumentative topics by examining the arguments on both sides of that argument or by proposing a compromise for competing sides of an argument. However, they are not asked to stake a position on a controversial topic and then defend that position for an audience that takes the opposing viewpoint. As a result, they do not have to deal with counterarguments to the position that those on the other side of the issue would take. (95-96)

The idea that the sophistication and subtlety of students' skills with argument will increase in college seems to make teachers less uncomfortable than they are with the developmental nature of other writing skills/concepts. There is much less debate or lamenting about students' abilities related to argument; we seem to have no problem accepting that there is a level of argumentation that will be best taught at college and that good high school writers will have a limited understanding of how to create sophisticated arguments. Students may still be confused by the use of "argument" to describe two different modes of writing, so it is still quite helpful for the WAC/WID teacher to know what expectations secondary writing teachers have when they teach argument.

In building on these expectations, college teachers can talk to students about what argument looks like in their discipline, demonstrating how writers in that discourse community use sources; how they find and use evidence; what constitutes good evidence; how they acknowledge and refute counter-arguments; what tones and styles are appropriate in argumentation; and, on a larger scale, what issues, ideas, and events are worth writing about in the discipline. The practice of argument, then, becomes an understanding of the nature and history of the discipline, an understanding of how knowledge is made within that discourse community.

Voice/Authority

When thinking about writing argumentatively in intellectual or academic discourse communities, we often assume and fail to discuss the importance of the writer's perception of her own role in the text she is writing. This idea of her role—her position, her relationship to her audience and her topic—is often encompassed in pre-college writing instruction in the term "voice." In college-level writing, particularly in the disciplines, we call upon writers to write with authority, with a certain attitude toward both the topic and the reader, and with a certain disciplinary style. Our entering students may not understand us when we talk about persona, authority, or role, but they have, in some sense, been introduced to these ideas in the term "voice," which, in secondary writing, may have been most closely associated with word choice and use of vivid detail.

Stephen Acker and Kay Halasek, in the *Journal of General Education*, comment on this shift in understanding; they interviewed writing teachers at both high school and college and found some disagreement about the nature and role of voice:

> In short, high school teachers typically encouraged students to create voice in personal essays (e.g., personal narratives or opinion pieces) but discouraged them from using that same 'voice' in more academic pieces (e.g., research papers). The distinction was not one generally made by college

teachers, who encouraged students to create voice in all of their academic writing. (9)

The difficulty in making this transition is probably directly related to the difference in the genres emphasized at each level, and the fact that the concept of "voice" most often taught at the pre-college level is drawn from the 6+1 Traits writing program, which describes voice from an almost entirely narrative and expressivist perspective, using measures of success such as "The writing sounds like you" or "Vivid descriptions make it seem like there's a real person behind the text" (PK-16).

Wendy Strachan describes the difference in voice/authority as related to a shifting understanding of how to use critical thinking and the students' own judgment and "a difference in perception of the relationship of students to their subject matter and, perhaps, in perceptions of learning and knowing" (143). One major cultural difference between high school writing and college writing is the notion of stance and relation of the writer to subject matter. Once students get to college, they will have to begin seeing "voice" as a sense of expertise in relation to their material and audience.

Kristen Dombek and Scott Herndon, in *Critical Passages: Teaching the Transition to College Composition*, note how this shift in understanding leads students to avoid using questions in their writing: "They may believe that academic thinking necessitates authority, and that asking too many questions destroys authority" (13). They insist that we need to help new students understand that questions do not undermine authority, to help them see that academic writing is "problem-motivated, rather than thesis-motivated" (19). We begin, they suggest, by helping students read good texts as "records of struggle" (19).

Edward White's "College-Level Writing and the Liberal Arts Tradition" offers similar advice: "College papers exist because writing is a student's chief means of learning, and college-level writing is usually designed to move students out of their comfort zone into new ways of thinking about complex matters" (298). Encouraging students to take risks with their writing is one of the perennial challenges first-year composition teachers face, but perhaps a greater understanding of how students perceive their role within the text, their "voice," will help both composition teachers and teachers of first-year students in all disciplines develop strategies for encouraging their development of an authoritative, problem-focused writing persona.

Conclusion

These three concepts—genre/format, argument, and authority/voice—identify specific elements of writing that incoming college students may have heard discussed in their high school classes and that they may have some understanding of. However, their high school understanding of these terms does not prepare them for how these concepts will be used in college-level writing, and may, in fact, hinder their ability to adapt to discipline-specific writing tasks. Frustrated WAC/WID practitioners may find that they cannot rely on students bringing writing skills and knowledge with them from high school because the students' understanding of these terms—the secondary teachers' definitions of these terms—are not sophisticated enough to allow a quick and easy transition into disciplinary discourses. The three elements of genre, argument, and voice all connect to a central shift away from "thinking like a student" toward thinking as a member of a discourse community. They are three parts of what is done when a given situation is rhetorically analyzed in order to determine what is right, what is best, and what elements of the audience need to be accounted for while writing. Genre conventions are strictly but subtly constructed by members of discourse communities; they are enforced by what is published and what is not, what is deemed successful and what is not, what is taught to newer members of the discourse community and what is not. The nature of both argument and voice are factors in these genre conventions, threads in the web of understanding the forces of appropriate discourse. A larger focus on genre conventions would encompass both argument and voice as writers learn how to relate to the other members of the discourse communities they enter. The key may be to begin, in all classes at college, to talk to students openly about disciplines as discourse communities and to emphasize the ways members of the discourse community talk to one another—how they make decisions about what is valued as evidence, style, organization, etc.

College writing teachers must acknowledge that students have been taught some of these elements as mere requirements of school writing—merely "what you're supposed to do" as a student writer. Teachers must build on students' previous practice as writers by helping them contextualize all of these choices as social—as choices grounded in a deep understanding of the conventions of a variety of academic and professional discourses. The skill of understanding how to join those communities—or even how to apprentice in them for one semester—has to come both from reading and analyzing texts within discourse communities and practicing writing those texts (or academic versions of those texts) which mimic the conventions and roles professional members of discourse communities adopt. To step back from the surface of any text to the "deep structure" of its place in the conversation of the discourse community requires some understanding of the community's purposes, history, place in society, scope and focus, mission, the past and present members, their goals, and the subtle shifts in emphasis that reveal the discourse community as a socially-constructed entity. In these ways, we can help each student break away from "thinking like a student" and begin "thinking like a writer."

Because teaching students how to join a professional and/or scholarly discourse community is complex and often exhausting, some college teachers choose not to do it and instead continue to teach a sort of hodge-podge generic academic discourse as is taught in high school, simply with more sophisticated expectations about depth of analysis and development of support. It takes members of any discourse community a long time to understand the "felt sense" of writing in that community, and we could argue that the knowledge is gained more than taught, but it is best gained by reading, discussing, and writing within that field, and being coached and responded to by more experienced members.

The complexity of this learning also makes it important for teachers at every level to adopt and teach a developmental approach to learning to write. Many voices in the research surrounding the transition from high school to college writing urge teachers who teach writing or use writing-to-learn methodologies to step back and adopt the attitude that writing is a skill that develops, not a one-time "problem" that can be learned and "taken care of" like riding a bicycle. Leann Carroll's *Rehearsing New Roles* is built on this premise, and she notes that current composition theorists "challenge the notion of a stable, unified 'writing ability' that can easily be measured by looking at isolated texts" (2). David Jolliffe agrees, recommending that all literacy advocates look skeptically at two propositions: "first, the notion that literacy is literacy is literacy, no matter what the context; and, second, the idea that once you've 'got' literacy, then you've 'got' it for life" (x).

Carroll urges us to change our thinking about how students learn to write, arguing that, "A developmental perspective also challenges the beliefs that students ought to know 'how to write' before they get to college" (26)—they cannot know "how to write" because there is no one way to do it, and writing ability continues to develop as writers encounter new discourse communities, audiences, and disciplines. If teachers can help their students become more aware of some of these salient features of discourses—of how questions about genre, argument, and voice are really questions about markers of belonging in particular discourse communities—students can learn disciplinary ways of writing. Understanding the ways these terms/concepts were used at the secondary level opens up ways for the WAC/WID teacher to build upon those foundations as they guide students toward a more rhetorical understanding of text and more community-situated discourses.

WORKS CITED

Acker, Stephen, and Kay Halasek. "Preparing High School Students for College-Level Writing: Using ePortfolio to Support the Transition." *Journal of General Education* 57.1 (2008): 1-14. Web.

Addison, Joanne, and Sharon James McGee. "Writing in High School/Writing in College: Research Trends and Future Directions." *College Composition and Communication*. 62.1 (Sept. 2010): 147-79. Print.

Alsup, Janet, and Michael Bernard-Donals. "The Fantasy of the 'Seamless Transition.'" Thompson, 115-35. Print.

Applebee, Arthur, and Judith Langer. "A Snapshot of Writing Instruction in Middle Schools and High Schools." *English Journal* 100.6 (2011): 14-27. Print.

Carroll, Lee Ann. *Rehearsing New Roles: How College Students Develop as Writers*. Carbondale, IL: Southern Illinois UP, 2002. Print.

Cobb, Victoria. "From Where They Sit: Stories of Students Making the Transition from High School Writing to College Writing." Diss. University of Texas, 2002. Austin. Web.

Dombek, Kristin, and Scott Herndon. *Critical Passages: Teaching the Transition to College Composition*. New York: Teacher's College Press, 2003. Print.

Donahue, Tiane. "Notes of a Humbled WPA: Dialogue with High School Colleagues." *Writing Instructor*. Sep. 2007. Web. 3 Nov. 2012.

Fanetti, Susan, Kathy M. Bushrow, and David L. DeWeese. "Closing the Gap Between High School Writing Instruction and College Writing Expectations." *English Journal* 99.4 (2010): 77-83. Print.

Farris, Christine. "Minding the Gap and Learning the Game: Differences That Matter between High School and College Writing." Hansen and Farris, 272-82. Print.

Graff, Gerald, and Cathy Birkenstein-Graff. "An Immodest Proposal for Connecting High School and College." *College Composition and Communication* 61.1 (Sept. 2009): W409-16. Print.

Hansen, Kristine, and Christine Farris, eds. *College Credit for Writing in High School: The "Taking Care of" Business*. Urbana, IL: NCTE, 2010. Print.

Jolliffe, David. "Forward: Tough Questions for Thoughtful Educators." Hansen and Farris, vii-xii. Print.

Jones, Joseph. "Muted Voices: High School Teachers, Composition, and the College Imperative." *Writing Instructor*. Sept. 2007. Web. 3 Nov. 2012.

Kittle, Peter. "It's Not the High School Teachers' Fault: An Alternative to the Blame Game." Sullivan, Tinberg, and Blau, 134-45. Print.

Kittle, Peter, and Rochelle Ramay. "Minding the Gaps: Public Genres and Academic Writing." Sullivan, Tinberg, and Blau, 98-118. Print.

Kiuhara, Sharlene, Steve Graham, and Leanne S. Hawken. "Teaching Writing to High School Students: A National Survey." *Journal of Educational Psychology* 101.1 (2009): 136-160. Web.

Lunsford, Ronald, John Kiser, and Deborah Coxwell-Teague. "Advanced Placement English and College Composition: A Comparison of Writing at the High School and First-Year College Levels." Sullivan, Tinberg, and Blau, 77-97. Print.

PK-16 Writing Partnership. *Writing Assessment and Instruction in the 21st Century: A Guidebook on Teaching and Assessing Writers Using the Six-Trait Writing Model in Content Areas*. Training Manual, PK-16 Writing Partnership: Staff Development in Writing Traits and Assessment. La Crosse: U of Wisconsin-La Crosse, 2004. Print.

Smit, David. "Practice, Reflection, and Genre." *Teaching Writing Teachers of High School English and First-year Composition.* Tremmel and Broz, 66-74. Print.

Strachan, Wendy. "Talking About the Transition: Dialogues Between High School and College Teachers." *Teaching Writing in High School and College: Conversations and Collaborations.* Ed. Thomas Thompson. Urbana, IL: NCTE, 136-50. Print.

Sullivan, Patrick, Howard Tinberg, and Sheridan Blau, eds. *What Is College-level Writing? Volume 2.* Urbana, IL: NCTE, 2010. Print.

Thompson, Thomas, ed. *Teaching Writing in High School and College: Conversations and Collaborations.* Urbana, IL: NCTE, 2002. Print.

Tremmel, Robert. "Introduction: Striking a Balance—Seeking a Discipline." Tremmel and Broz, 1-15. Print.

Tremmel, Robert, and William Broz, eds. *Teaching Writing Teachers of High School English and First-year Composition.* Portsmouth, NH: Heinemann, 2002. Print.

White, Edward M. "College-Level Writing and the Liberal Arts Tradition." Sullivan, Tinberg, and Blau, 295-99. Print.

Yancey, Kathleen Blake. "Responding Forward." Sullivan, Tinberg, and Blau, 300-11. Print.

Spectators at Their Own Future: Creative Writing Assignments in the Disciplines and the Fostering of Critical Thinking

ALEXANDRIA PEARY

OF THE THREE ARMS OF DISCOURSE identified by James Britton—expressive, transactional, and poetic—the poetic, the language of creative writing, has to date received the least coverage in the pedagogy of writing across the curriculum (WAC). In this article, I explore James Britton's and Art Young's notion of how moving away from expressive and toward poetic discourse (by working in the forms of creative discourse) evokes the spectator stance and enhances critical thinking in the disciplines. I discuss one creative writing across the curriculum (CWAC) assignment that utilizes that continuum between expressive and poetic discourse: it asks students to compose first-person short fictional pieces set five to ten years into the future in which they appear as characters on the job in their future professions. In engaging in this fictional narrative about professional activity, students (aviation and computer science majors) crafted a plot that allowed them to use course content to work through a particular set of problems they might encounter in the workplace. Students are transformed into characters inside their poetic objects and thus can contemplate themselves as professionals. They become spectators at their own futures, and in gazing ahead, they can follow and alter the trajectory of their assumptions. As a result, the spectatorship in this type of assignment can provide a stage for engagement with critical thinking in courses in the disciplines.

The Move from Expressive to Poetic Discourse

According to Britton and Young, discourse occurs on a continuum whereby expressive discourse has the mobility to inch more or less close to either transactional or poetic discourse. Expressive discourse is the arguably more natural mode, resembling ordinary talk (Britton, *Language* 177). Children's writing, freewriting, journaling, or emails are examples of expressive discourse. Poetic writing, or creative writing, in contrast, is an aesthetic artifact—it's "MAKING something with language" through a knowledge of the conventions of the creative genres and it hopefully evokes an appreciative spectator stance in its reader (Britton "Spectator" 158-59 and 170-71). Young provides a close-up view of that spectrum between expressive and poetic discourse. That is, Young posits an intermediary point between the two poles such that some texts are closer to the intermediary expressive stage—"where the writing tends to the poetic but is not 'shaped'"—and other texts move closer to the poetic—and thus increasingly resemble creative writing or a polished literary product ("Considering" 79).

The protean nature of expressive discourse is important because it is through the polishing of the expressive into the more formal discourse of the poetic that "spectatorship" or critical thinking in the disciplines can occur. Working toward more formal creative writing affords benefits to learning since the "experience of writing in poetic form transforms thought and assists the writer in achieving the personal (evaluating new experience) and social (imaginative empathy and insight) purposes" (Young, "Considering" 83). The devices of creative writing change how students express course content, yielding "new perceptions of experience" and "the necessary distance for the individual involved in the self-examination of values" (83). Britton calls this critical stance the "spectator role" and proposed that poetic discourse is distinctive for the way in which it allows its author to become a spectator to his or her experience. When individuals recount a story—even as ordinary gossip—they are no longer a part of the event being described: they are evaluating their experience from a cognitive distance. Citing D. W. Harding, Britton describes the impact of this spectator stance:

> In participation we evaluate, necessarily, in preparation for action; but "detached evaluative responses [that is, those of the spectator] though less intense, tend to be more widely comprehensive than the evaluation which preceded participation." ... The spectator, then, freed from the necessity to act, to meet the social demands made upon a participant, uses his freedom to *evaluate* more broadly, more amply. (109)

The "active but disinterested" mindset that comes from working with poetic discourse is less possible with transactional discourse (such as a job cover letter or an informational report), in which the writer is still a participant in the sense that he or she seeks in some fashion to cause change vis-à-vis the reader (land the job, change an opinion, stimulate action) (Young, "Writing" 161).

Spectatorship positions learners to course material such that critical thinking can be initiated and maintained. By becoming a spectator, students gain a valuable critical distance which allows them to engage in the foundational activities of the critical thinking coveted in higher education, activities which John C. Bean identified as interaction with a problem, identification and critique of assumptions, and a dialogic interchange with the ideas of others (2-3). While composing creative writing, students are able to adopt alternative points-of-view, give consideration to context, and search for multiple possible outcomes or conclusions. Narrative, for example, has been attributed with expanded lines of inquiry for students learning code in an introductory programming course at The Robert Gordon University in Scotland. Rote learning was replaced with the "divergent nature of narrative – the fact that it is possible to imagine an endless series of scenarios which have the same set of core structural features but differ completely in narrative content" (McDermott et al. 39). With CWAC, students are also called upon to dialogically reflect on concepts and their greater context, on the interaction of self and larger society—a critical thinking capacity already noted in some disciplines. For instance, the field of sociology has designated a term, coined by C. Wright Mills in 1959, for the blend of imaginative and critical thinking that entails seeing the self in and as shaped by societal context: the "sociological imagination." In computer science, "the psychology of computer programming" refers to a sub-field which investigates programming as a social activity, not merely a matter of technical expertise, but rather one profoundly affected by the interaction of individual and group psychologies (Weinberg 33). Other fields of study could benefit from this sort of formalized understanding and application of the imagination, and CWAC can assist with this endeavor. The critical distance made possible by creative writing is hardly passive because in telling a story that addresses course concepts, for instance, students must literally activate or animate those concepts—exploring the complexities of the ideas through characters, plot, imagery, and so forth. Creative writing accentuates one of the properties which Janet Emig identified as unique to writing overall: it fuels learning because it is "enactive": we learn by doing—and writing helps us "do" (124-25). As a result of working with poetic discourse, students can't hide their level of comprehension behind what can become the bric-a-brac of conventional academic assignments—in-text citations, paraphrase, and so forth: instead, students engaged in writing creatively in the disciplines need to activate and extend their knowledge.

Creative writing assignments can be used throughout the curriculum for the promotion of discipline-specific learning. Young has assigned creative writing to science, business, and engineering majors in literature courses, but he maintains that creative writing not be limited to literature courses and instead be tailored to the content of courses from across the curriculum ("Considering" 87-88). Young's facilitation of such assignments in disciplines including psychology, philosophy, biology, architecture, and chemistry is documented in *Teaching and Learning Creatively: Inspirations and Reflections*, the 2006 edited collection on the poetry-across-the-curriculum initiative at Clemson University. Describing the application of creative writing in an Abnormal Psychology class, Young and co-authors state that "writing a poem is an exercise in problem finding, a skill essential to creative work in both the arts and the sciences" (Connor-Greene et al., "Poetry" 215). Patrick Bahls has developed poetry assignments in mathematics both for general education courses and ones taken by math majors. For Bahls, poetry provides students with an alternative discourse to the potentially daunting terminology of mathematics by allowing students to explore math in personal and jargon-free ways. As a result, general education students gain the comfort of using genres familiar to them from the qualitative work of their majors, and underclass math majors gain the confidence that may persuade them to continue with the major (*Student Writing* 120; "Math and Metaphor" 76-79). In fact, the functionality of CWAC to promote discipline-specific learning is evinced in its appearance in pedagogy journals in a range of disciplines, including *The Journal of Education for Business; Teaching Sociology; The Journal of Medical Humanities; Journal of General Internal Medicine; Families, Systems, and Health; Journal of Chemical Education;* and *Journal of Health Psychology.*

Creative writing assignments set in the future, including ones in which students become spectators of their future professional lives, compel students to engage in inductive thinking since what students are creating could be considered extended hypothetical examples. Story-telling was categorized by Aristotle as a type of inductive-based example: "But of examples, there are two species; for one species of example is the quoting of real matters of fact which have actually taken place; another is fabricating them yourself; and of this method, one species is illustration, the other fable" (170). Narrative, as an extended hypothetical example, requires students to understand course concepts as a type of observed evidence sufficiently enough to make a credible prediction, in fiction, about the future of those concepts. *Given x, y, and z, what could possibly happen* is a different cognitive act from simply restating what already has happened and what is already known. Exemplification transforms a nebulous or abstract discussion into something more concrete because it requires the introduction of evidence (Wästerfors and Holsanova 520, 547). At the same time, examples can be understood as "a point of departure" from reality, and one type of example, the "virtual example," is a way to increase comprehension (Wästerfors and Holsanova 519, 546). It is precisely that capacity to diverge from the known and not only to move into but to *illuminate* the unknown that is one of the functions of the poetic discourse. As Britton, again citing H.G. Widdowson, explains, the poetic results in text "independent of a social context and expressive of a reality other than that which is sanctioned by convention . . . literature must be deviant as a discourse" ("Spectator" 160). As aberration, such a perspective allows the student to engage critically with disciplinary knowledge: "To exemplify what never happens may in an inverse way illuminate what really happens" (Wästerfors and Holsanova

546). Through fiction assignments, for instance, Nancy Welch gets her students to use inductive thinking as a way to evaluate critically assumptions about the present or to perform "sideshadowing." Sideshadowing means thinking critically about the present moment such that any future outcome doesn't seem inevitable (Welch 120).

Futuristic Narrative Assignment in the Disciplines

In the creative writing assignment described in this article, students used the genre of short fiction to design a futuristic event in which they are participants. Specifically, students were asked to write a first-person short story in which they appear as a character in a narrative that takes place in the future and on the job (in plane, airport, air traffic control tower, cubicle, conference room, cafeteria) over a single work day or through two separate scenes, using flashbacks and flashforwards. None of the students were English or creative writing majors. The assignments were presented to aviation majors enrolled in an upper-level cockpit resource management course in their junior or senior year, to sociology of gender students, and to computer science majors in a 300-level software engineering course.[1] The goal of these short stories was to manifest course content; rather than restating the technology, terminology and concepts of a field of study, students needed to show those elements of the course *in action*, encapsulated in a plot in which they were a main character. Through dialogue, detail, and plot, students implicitly demonstrated course concepts including situational awareness, mission analysis, and interpersonal communication (aviation); occupational segregation and intersectionality (sociology); and moving target, Miller's Law, and cognitive dissonance (computer science) without specifically referencing those concepts.

This assignment builds off of other CWAC assignments in the disciplines that require students to investigate disciplinary concepts and professional practices through imaginary or on-the-job scenarios. In Doug Laufer and Rick Crosser's series of scenario-based CWAC assignments in undergraduate accounting and tax courses, students are asked to contemplate various problematic situations. In one, students are told to pretend they are "a sole proprietor tax practitioner" on April 14, the day before Tax Day; upon visiting a client's home office while the client is away on business travel, the student/tax practitioner notes the luxury of the client's office furnishings and realizes the furnishings need to be quickly included in the tax filing. The student is told to write a letter that can be faxed to the imaginary client addressing the need to include the office furnishing in the April 15 filing (89). In another CWAC project, Daniel Moore asks business students to play a role by composing reports and memos with the goal of adopting a range of perspectives and crafting an appropriate voice. While Laufer, Crosser, and Moore require students to imagine themselves in a future situation of professionalism (already employed as a CPA in a firm), the resulting text is in a genre typical of that profession (tax filing, memos, and in another of Laufer and Crosser's assignments, a section of an intermediate accounting textbook). The CWAC project described in this article builds off these approaches by asking students to cast themselves as characters in first-person fiction rather than compose a text in response to an imaginary situation. Specifically, the narrative of the first-person fiction project discussed in this article allows students to investigate the complex day-to-day activity of their professions rather than focusing on the disciplinary conventions of a workplace genre and writing a pretend transactional document. It is a different cognitive challenge from asking: *Do you know how you would write client correspondence if you were a practicing accountant?*

Typically, the first-person fiction assignments required that students cast themselves as professionals five to ten years after obtaining their undergraduate degree, using an imaginary setting occurring in the workplace. For instance, aviation students displayed cockpit resource management techniques as well as knowledge of flight technology in a working day in their lives as commercial pilots. Sociology and computer science students in two other courses, sociology of gender and software engineering, also described a day-in-their-life ten years hence but this time using multiple settings—home, commute, and free-time activities as well as the workplace. For the computer science students, this thinking was triggered by the first prompt given to them during an in-class brainstorming session to start the project:

> Freewrite for five minutes, jotting down any phrases, specific details, imagery, terminology in a list format—phrases and sentences which come to mind when asked: *Imagine yourself five years from now. What is your ideal professional experience in a day-in-the-life scenario as a programmer five years into the future?* For instance, what sort of company do you want to work for? What's the name of the company? Where is it located? Where are *you* located (if you're telecommuting)? Write down anything which comes to mind.

Students imagined their job as a Human Resource director or encountering their new next-door neighbor, a stay-at-home dad with a high-powered wife and a Baby Bjorn strapped across his chest, toddler toys spewing over the driveway. They wrote about working as a younger co-pilot faced with a lack of clear communication with an older and higher-ranking pilot. They created workplace scenarios as programmers in which a fictional client's project is positively affected by the physical arrangement of the workplace (a Google HQ-style gourmet cafeteria and a room to practice yoga) or hampered by a change in the group dynamic (a colleague undergoing a marital separation).

Implementing and Grading the Project

The CWAC team-taught ventures I describe in this article were all tied to a substantial portion of students' final course grades—ranging from twelve to thirty-five percent—and involved multiple drafts and a workshop session. These ventures entailed a single major writing project inside another faculty member's course in the disciplines—and not the full-semester creative writing focus as described by Nancy Welch and Sandra Young. In this case, the amount of collaboration with the instructor from the discipline was fairly high in order to help the students engage each of the parts of the writing process. Through this sort of intensive collaboration and the provision of this support from a rhetoric and composition/WAC specialist, CWAC assignments can become a possibility for most faculty across the disciplines. That said, not every CWAC project requires this level of collaboration—as evinced in the soloist successes of Patrick Bahls and David Zehr.

For example, one recent collaborative venture, in the above-mentioned 300-level software engineering course, entailed two initial meetings with the professor from the computer science department to discuss ways in which the CWAC project could address his learning outcomes for his course. Using this information, I designed prompts that were extensive and specific, the professor provided feedback on these prompts, and we developed a teaching plan for my visit to his class. On the day of the classroom visit, the professor and I team-taught the heuristics, allowing students in-class time to develop freewritten answers to them. I returned to the programming class a second time to co-facilitate a workshop session in which students provided peer feedback as well as engaged in in-class revision on their own drafts using prompts designed to address certain content areas and fiction-writing techniques (see Appendix A). While not every WAC facilitator may opt for using peer review, I find it to be an invaluable part of the writing process for its propagation of possibilities about form and content, providing students with a larger range of revision ideas than can be provided by instructor-readers.

The extent to which creative writing assignments should be graded varies between CWAC practitioners. Art Young, for instance, has consistently advised against grading these assignments in order to keep them low-stakes and informal: "I do not grade or write evaluative comments on the poems. . . . Many people are already anxious at the prospect of writing a poem because it may be an unfamiliar task, and concern about a grade may heighten anxiety and reduce creative exploration" ("Poetry" 217). Patrick Bahls grades drafts but only as a measurement of effort: "in order to keep the stakes low and to nurture a safe environment in which students could feel free to explore, students were graded only on whether or not they completed each stage of the assignment" ("Math" 80).

In the CWAC project for the software engineering course, students were not expected to produce high-quality literature but were instead evaluated—and only in part—on whether they paid sufficient attention to various creative writing devices and whether they had sufficiently engaged in the writing process. Students had several deadlines for drafts, all of which carried a portion of the project's final grade: they sent us their initial brainstorming, an outline or two-page draft, their peer feedback on workshop day, a revised draft, and the final draft. Fifty percent of the grade for the project was calculated by whether they had completed the different stages of the process in a timely fashion. The remaining fifty percent of the grade, determined by both instructors, was based on students' use of descriptive techniques (contemporary and technological detail, imagery, sensory information, setting) and the development of a two-scene narrative timeline (involving two separate moments in time in order to better show change in the plot and disciplinary content). Students were evaluated on how well they explored the following areas specific to the field of software engineering, doing so largely through character development and dialogue: teamwork dynamics, internal/group communication dynamics, and external communication dynamics. Our grading rubric for the final draft was modified from Patrick Bahls' *Student Writing in the Quantitative Disciplines* to designate percentage points for each category of effort and to link ten percent of the grade to use of description and ten percent to use of narrative (See Appendix B).[2]

Critical Thinking Through the Development of a Futuristic Plot

Through a composing and revising process, with this futuristic first-person fiction assignment, students eventually transitioned from early brainstorming and freewriting work, which was closer to the intermediary-expressive stage, to the poetic discourse of a polished story. Although students were briefly introduced to the assignment and told they would be writing a final draft in the genre of a short story, initial tasks resembled more expressive than fully formed poetic discourse. The first set of prompts given during the initial in-class session asked students to begin drawing personal connections with material covered during the semester as possible application to creative writing without having to actually utilize creative writing devices. For instance, students were asked to brainstorm for characters who would become members on fictional software project teams, listing information about each character's age, gender, name, personality type, race, work experience, and personality type. Other creative writing devices students were asked to brainstorm about included setting, time line, and characters (not team members but instead supervisors and clients). Students linked course concepts and creative writing devices in an outline format for their rough draft and began trying out creative writing devices in their second draft. As they composed that second draft and revised according to responses obtained during a peer workshop and from instructor-provided revision prompts, students increased their engagement with poetic discourse by working hands-on with creative writing devices.

At all stages of this assignment, fictional narrative served as a mechanism through which students could articulate course knowledge in their discipline. According to James Kalmbach and William Powers, narration promotes comprehension because it requires the careful sorting through of detail: "Narrators must sort out from such quantity of detail only those events which seem important or significant to the story at hand.... This process of selection is a form of understanding" (101). To compose the speculative fiction assignment, students needed to review in their minds concepts covered in the course, critically consider and select which concepts they would realistically encounter in a day at work ten years in the future, and determine how to relate those concepts to other matters—both to fictional elements and additional course material.

In addition to organizing detail, narrative also asks students to make meaning through the establishment of a time line (Peterson-Gonzalez). To help the computer science students develop a narrative, we asked:

> Thinking of the first day of starting a new project, design a straight narrative time line for that day. When will you start depicting that work day? What will be the highlights? Make sure that those highlights display a quantity of professional information and course concepts. In a three-minute brainstorm, come up with four different moments in that straight time line of a day at work starting the project.

Students crafted a variety of time lines with scenes including lunch meetings, the news of a colleague's involvement in a car accident, presentations to clients, and post-project celebrations all of which (due to the nature of their future profession) centered around the sine qua non of successful software engineering—whether the programmers met the client's deadline. As students worked with one element of narrative, flashback, they were able to consider critically the impact of a particular strategy or element in programming.

In a prompt, students were asked:

> Another plot development: on the first day of the project, something about it reminds you of a previous project in which there arose a problem in requirements. What happened back then? Were the goals not clear? Were there too many goals or were the goals changed in some way? In a three-minute brainstorm/freewrite, create details and use this later as a flashback inside your story.

One student developed a flashback to explore the problems that arise when programmers fail to use layperson's terminology when communicating with a client:

> I remembered years ago when we were just starting up. We met with the client, asked some questions and then assumed that we knew better, that the client is dumb, and we were the smart ones. As a result, we implemented features which the client didn't need and missed the features that the client actually needed. We lost the client; he refused to pay for something half-finished that he didn't need.

In his story, the student tries to imagine the point-of-view of the client and how foreign the software engineering environment may be to her: "Next day, Ms. Smith walked in our office staring as if she was looking at the landscape of another planet [though] the area was nothing special, some workstations scattered around a huge round desk and strange symbols filling writing boards hanging on the wall." He shows himself remembering the lesson of that flashback and avoiding a repeat of the mistake by asking the client about intended audience, priority features, and future applications of her commissioned program. Overall, this type of work with narration helped students engage in inductive thinking: if they followed one programming method, what would occur, given the fictional scenario—and what modifications would their team of characters need to make in order to meet the deadline for the software project? Through increasingly more refined work with poetic devices, students were able to critique their assumptions about the human dynamic inherent in software engineering. An early prompt challenged students with the following interpersonal scenario:

> There's something "up" with one of the team members. What is it? Has something drastic changed in their personal life? Has their attitude to their job changed, and if so, why/how so? Or are they a brand-new team member? In a three-minute brainstorm or freewrite: Develop an image: something about their work space and some gesture or small action they do which suggests their status. Use this detail later inside your story.

Students came up with disgruntled colleagues who are secretly on the job market, pregnant colleagues, colleagues with bad backs, colleagues distracted by wedding plans, arrogant Ivy League degree-holding colleagues, and colleagues undergoing marital problems. As they developed drafts, students showed themselves examining their assumptions about their colleagues by depicting themselves negotiating or confiding with other characters.

One course concept examined through creative methods was Brook's Law: the phenomena in which adding programming personnel to a team because a product is falling behind schedule has the effect of making the product's delivery even later. To that end, one student depicts himself as technical development manager in his branch office having to stick by his decision to use pair programming (only two people per group) when a subordinate comes to him requesting additional teammates to ease the stress of a deadline.

Later on, through revision prompts on the advanced draft of this project, students were asked to identify which course concepts were being implicitly conveyed in a passage from their drafts and to think of two additional ways in which those concepts could more substantially influence the plot. They then extended that exploration of course concepts through additional character or plot details or by allowing the workplace setting to play a factor in those concepts and in the imaginary team's performance.

Pilot Study Findings and Conclusion

In the pilot study I conducted in my most recent CWAC venture, computer science students were administered a Likert scale-based survey before starting the speculative fiction project and again after completing the project. The sample was limited (only nine of the twenty-four students were present on the class meeting in which the post-survey was distributed), and the results cannot be claimed to be generalizable from this particular instance of CWAC research. However, the pre- and post-test surveys suggest improvement in student perception of the import of social factors on programming including client interactions and the impact of the workplace setting. The most significant change in student perspective from prior to the assignment to after the assignment's completion is evident in students' responses to the survey statement, "I believe that successful programming depends as much on social and psychological factors as it does on technological knowledge." Students' responses moved from Agree to Strongly Agree and from 6.8 to 8.1 on the Likert scale (see Appendix C).

When creative writing is construed as merely a matter of that customary line-up of introductory, intermediate, and advanced craft workshops taken chiefly by English majors, there's a missed opportunity for a unique mode of learning. As individuals create any poetic object—whether a poem, story, memoir, play, and so forth—they concentrate on manipulating various literary devices to make that verbal object. Due to a focus on line breaks, iambic pentameter, or an omniscient narrator, students gain an objectivity on course material and a distance from their own views of disciplinary concepts. Creative writing could be used powerfully more often across the curriculum in order to advance critical thinking in the disciplines. The futuristic narrative assignment described in this article helps students speculate on their lives, their majors, their professions—not to mention the course material studied all semester. Creative writing in the disciplines allows course material to become a vivid detail, part of a tricky plot, be batted around by complex characters—all part of a complex critical act of asking "what if?"

Notes

1. For a version of this assignment for a non-technical class, see my co-authored article with Laurie Gordy, "Bringing Creativity into the Classroom: Using Sociology to Write First-Person Fiction."

2. Bahls's rubric does not discuss grade points or percentages, indicative of the usage of the rubric in low-stakes tasks. His rubric is intended to help an instructor identify a student's "level of achievement" with a creative task. Bahls does suggest, however, that the rubric could be altered for the purposes of grading (*Student Writing* 125).

* Many thanks to Roman Burdakov, Laurie Gordy, Joe Kasprzyk, Viktar Kavalenka, Weining Lv, Ken Mahoney, Shirley Phillips, Tom Teller, and Jack Zaharoff for trying out and sustaining creative writing-based WAC in their classrooms and their writing.

WORKS CITED

Aristotle. *Treatise on Rhetoric*. Trans. Thomas Hobbes. London: G. Bell: 1880.

Bahls, Patrick. "Math and Metaphor: Using Poetry to Teach College Mathematics." *WAC Journal* 20 (2009): 75-90.

—. *Student Writing in the Quantitative Disciplines: A Guide for College Faculty*. San Francisco: Jossey-Bass, 2012.

Bean, John C. *Engaging Ideas: The Professor's Guide to Integrating Writing, Critical Thinking, and Active Learning in the Classroom*. San Francisco: Jossey Bass, 1996.

Britton, James. *Language and Learning*. Coral Gables, FL: U of Miami P, 1970.

—. "Spectator Role and the Beginnings of Writing." *What Writers Know: The Language, Process, and Structure of Written Discourse*. Ed. Marty Nystrand. New York: Academic, 1982. 149-69.

Britton, James, et al. *The Development of Writing Abilities (11-18)*. London: MacMillan, 1975.

Connor-Greene, Patricia A., Janice W. Murdoch, Art Young, and Catherine Paul. "Poetry: It's Not Just for English Class Anymore." *Teaching of Psychology* 32.4 (2005): 215-21.

Connor-Greene, Patricia A., Catherine Mobley, Catherine E. Paul, Jerry A. Waldvogel, Liz Wright, and Art Young. *Teaching and Learning Creatively: Inspirations and Reflections*. West Lafayette, IN: Parlor Press, 2006.

Elbow, Peter. "High Stakes and Low Stakes in Assigning and Responding to Writing." *Everyone Can Write: Essays Toward a Hopeful Theory of Writing and Teaching Writing*. Oxford: Oxford UP, 2000: 351-59.

Emig, Janet. "Writing as a Mode of Learning." *College Composition and Communication* 28.2 (May 1977): 122-28.

Estes, Gisela B., Barbara Lopez-Mayhew, and Marie- Therese Gardner. "Writing in the Foreign Languages Department." *WAC Journal* 9 (Aug. 1998): 68-81.

Gordy, Laurie, and Alexandria Peary. "Bringing Creativity into the Classroom: Using Sociology to Writer First-Person Fiction." *Teaching Sociology* 33.4 (Oct. 2005): 396-402.

Jennings, Lisa. "Making the Connection: A 'Lived History' Assignment in an Upper-Division German Course." *WAC Journal* 16 (Sept. 2005): 61-69.

Kalmbach, James, and William Powers. "Shaping Experience: Narration and Understanding." *Language Connections: Writing and Reading Across the Curriculum*. Ed. Toby Fulwiler and Art Young. Urbana, IL: NCTE, 1982. 99-106.

Kerr, Lisa. "More than Words: Applying the Discipline of Literary Creative Writing to the Practice of Reflective Writing in Health Care Education." *Journal of Medical Humanities* 31 (2010): 295-301.

Laufer, Doug, and Rick Crosser. "The 'Writing-Across-the-Curriculum' Concept in Accounting and Tax Courses." *Journal of Education for Business* 66.2 (Nov./Dec. 1990): 83-88.

Lopez-Mayhew, Barbara. "Writing in the Foreign Languages Department." *WAC Journal* 9 (Aug. 1998): 68-81.

Mayers, Tim. *(Re)Writing Craft: Composition, Creative Writing, and the Future of English Studies*. Pittsburgh: U of Pittsburgh P, 2005.

McDermott, R., G. Eccleston, and G. Brindley. "More Than a Good Story: Can You Really Teach Programming Through Storytelling?" *Innovations in Teaching and Learning in Information and Computer Science* 7.1 (2008): n. pag. Web. 5 May 2012.

Mills, C. Wright. *The Sociological Imagination*. London: Oxford UP, 1959.

Moore, Daniel P. "Exploring Voice in Business Writing." *WAC Journal* 5 (May 1994): 39-44.

Perkins, Ray, and Dan Kervick. "Teaching Writing and Teaching Philosophy." *WAC Journal* 9 (Aug. 1998): 46-51.

Petersen, Meg. "The Atomic Weight of Metaphor: Writing Poetry Across the Curriculum." *WAC Journal* 12 (May 2001): 97-100.

Peterson-Gonzalez, Meg. "In Defense of Storytelling." *WAC Journal* 6 (Aug. 1995): 63-70.

Reisman, Ana B., Helena Hansen, and Asghar Rastegar. "The Craft of Writing: A Physician-Writer's Workshop for Resident Physicians." *Journal of General Internal Medicine* 21 (2006): 1109-1111.

Shapiro, Johanna, and Howard Stein. "Poetic License: Writing Poetry as a Way for Medical Students to Examine their Professional Relational Systems." *Families, Systems, and Health* 23 (2005): 278-92.

Thomas, Elizabeth, and Anne Mulvey. "Using the Arts in Teaching and Learning: Building Student Capacity for Community-Based Work in Health Psychology. " *Journal of Health Psychology* 13.2 (2008): 239-50.

Vittum, Henry E., and Robert S. Miller. "Writing in the Capstone Experience: Psychology Encounters Literature." *WAC Journal* 4 (Apr. 1993): 164-78.

Weinberg, Gerald M. *The Psychology of Computer Programming.* New York: Van Nostrand, 1971.

Welch, Nancy. "No Apology: Challenging the 'Uselessness' of Creative Writing." *JAC: A Journal of Composition Theory* 19 (1999): 117-34.

Wästerfors, David, and Jana Holsanova. "Examples as Crucial Arguments in Discourse on 'Others.'" *Text* 25.4 (2005): 519-54.

Young, Art. "Considering Values: The Poetic Function of Language." *Language Connections: Writing and Reading Across the Curriculum.* Ed. Toby Fulwiler and Art Young. Urbana, IL: NCTE, 1982. 77-97.

—. "Writing Across and Against the Curriculum." *Writing Across the Curriculum: A Critical Sourcebook.* Ed. Terry Myers Zawacki and Paul M. Rogers. Boston: Bedford St. Martin's, 2012. 158-67.

Young, Sandra. "Beyond 'Hot Lips' and 'Big Nurse': Creative Writing and Nursing." *Composition Studies* 33.1 (Spring 2005): 75-91.

Zehr, David. "Buffy and Elvis: The Sequel." *WAC Journal* 6 (Aug. 1995): 15-22.

Appendix A: Peer Workshop Handout

Instructions: Exchange drafts with another student. Read through the entire draft without making notes; read the draft a second time keeping the below questions in mind. Provide feedback to the other student by answering (in detail) the below questions.

Note: 10% of your grade on this project is based on the quality of your responses on the other student's draft. Supply careful, detailed advice.

1. What are the best attributes of this draft?
2. Where do you want more material?
3. Ask at least 3 questions concerning the project and/or company depicted in the story. What sorts of detail would better help you understand the student's workplace experience? Another way of thinking about this: if you were just talking to the student about his job, what are 3 questions you'd naturally have about his workplace experience?
4. Pick 2-3 scenes in the draft which involve an interaction between 2 or more characters. (One of the characters could include the student, so a first-person "I.") *Can you tell which course concepts are being implied through the scenes?* List those course concepts and explain how you know from the descriptions and interactions of the characters that those concepts are being implied.

5. How could the student do a stronger job of implying those concepts in question #4? To that end, give them advice on the following:
    a. Gestures
    b. Physical descriptions
    c. Dialogue
    d. Setting details
6. Let's take the character interactions a step deeper now. In question #4, Characters A, B, and C do something, suggesting that Z (course concept—something about the psychology of programming & teamwork) is going on. *Because Z is going on, what happens NEXT in the plot? How does Z affect the programming project?* Give the student 2 suggestions as to how each of the course concepts you identified in your answer to question #4 could *affect what proceeds*.

Appendix B: Rubric for Final Draft

Criterion	Not Met (0-3 points)	Partially Met (4-7 points)	Fully Met (8-10 points)
Project demonstrates student's OVERALL understanding of teamwork dynamics in software engineering 10% OF GRADE	Student's project demonstrates no (or poor) overall understanding of teamwork dynamics	Student's project demonstrates partial understanding of overall teamwork dynamics, but some aspects remain elusive	Student's project demonstrates solid understanding of overall teamwork dynamics (with only minor errors)
Project demonstrates student's understanding of course concepts: *internal/group communication issues in software engineering* 10% OF GRADE	Student's project demonstrates no (or poor) understanding of related concepts	Student's project demonstrates partial understanding, but some aspects of course concepts remain elusive	Student's project demonstrates solid understanding of course concepts (with only minor errors)
Project demonstrates student's understanding of course concepts: *external communication issues in software engineering* 10% OF GRADE	Student's project demonstrates no (or poor) understanding of related concepts	Student's project demonstrates partial understanding, but some aspects of course concepts remain elusive	Student's project demonstrates solid understanding of course concepts (with only minor errors)
Project demonstrates student's effort to achieve literary or aesthetic merit (whether or not this merit is fully realized): *descriptive techniques* 10% OF GRADE	Student's work shows no or little effort (it is sloppy and hastily formed)	Student's work shows some effort (some care is taken in its crafting; improvements have been made on a rough draft)	Student's work shows considerable effort and attention to detail (it is polished; effort is made to ensure aesthetic appeal)

Criterion	Not Met (0-3 points)	Partially Met (4-7 points)	Fully Met (8-10 points)
Project demonstrates student's effort to achieve literary or aesthetic merit (whether or not this merit is fully realized): *narrative techniques* 10% OF GRADE	Student's work shows no or little effort (it is sloppy and hastily formed)	Student's work shows some effort (some care is taken in its crafting; improvements have been made on a rough draft)	Student's work shows considerable effort and attention to detail (it is polished; effort is made to ensure aesthetic appeal)

Appendix C: Pre- and Post-Survey Results

N=9

Strongly Disagree   Agree   Strongly Agree

1   2   3   4   5   6   7   8   9   10

	Pre-Survey Average of Responses	Post-Survey Average of Responses	Amount of Change
I know how to write a quality fictional narrative.	6.5	7.5	1.0
I know how to put important course concepts in my own words.	6.9	7.9	1.0
I have confidence in my ability to write a fictional narrative that incorporates important course concepts.	6.9	7.7	0.8
I believe that successful programming depends as much on social and psychological factors as it does on technological knowledge.	6.8	8.1	1.3
I believe there is an important relation between physical work space and social structure of programming.	7.7	8.5	0.8
I believe it is important not to assume that a client shares the same understanding of programming terminology that I do.	8.5	9.3	0.8

	Pre-Survey Average of Responses	Post-Survey Average of Responses	Amount of Change
I believe that creative writing can increase my understanding of course content.	6.2	7.0	0.8
I believe that creative writing can increase my interest in course content.	5.5	6.4	0.9

Joe Harris: Teaching Writing Via the Liberal Arts

CAROL RUTZ

ONE OF THE PLEASURES of interviewing one's professional colleagues is the chance to present a candid and approachable picture of a well-known scholar. Some of us come across majestically in our scholarly prose—a contrast to the informal, down-to-earth selves we present in person. Such is not the case for Joe Harris, the kind colleague who cheerfully submitted to an interview for this issue. Joe's lucid prose is the real thing—a reflection of his personal presence. If there is a difference, it lies in a bit more overt humor in face-to-face conversation. Otherwise, the author of works that include *A Teaching Subject: Composition since 1966* and my personal favorite, *Rewriting: How to Do Things with Texts*, exhibits the kind of wordsmithery that trades polysyllabic obfuscation for transparent, idiomatic prose that is always informed and interesting sans foppish erudition. (That last phrase would be the kind of thing Joe would never write. Not ever. Thank goodness.)

Joe earned his BA at Haverford College and his MA and PhD at New York University. After a few short stints teaching at various institutions, he settled in at the University of Pittsburgh for eleven years, departing for Duke University in 1999. He is currently an associate professor of English, having spent his first decade at Duke as director of what is now known as the Thompson Writing Program, which employs postdocs from a variety of disciplines. One might characterize the program as writing across the curriculum (WAC) in action. Because the interview touches on Joe's work at Duke as well as his considerable experience as an editor, I trust readers will find details about all of that rendered much better in Joe's words than in anything I could provide here.

The following evolved through e-mail correspondence and an extended conversation at the Conference on College Composition and Communication (CCCC) in St. Louis in March of 2012.

Carol Rutz: If I remember correctly, our first conversation occurred at least ten years ago in an elevator in Charlotte, North Carolina, and the subject was Jesse James. Do I have that right?

Joe Harris: Yes! As I recall, you were wearing a nametag that said you were from Northfield, Minnesota. Recalling a boyhood filled with stories and movies about cowboys and Indians, outlaws and lawmen, I blurted out that I had always wanted to visit Northfield, which we all know as the site of the James/Younger gang's final, disastrous bank heist. A few years later you invited me to talk with your faculty at Carleton College (it turns out, also located in Northfield, but strangely omitted from the tales of the James gang) and, as a special treat, took me afterwards to a storefront museum commemorating the failed raid. I was very happy.

CR: I remember your happiness, which was later exhibited with your trademark wit when you posted autopsy photos of the hapless gang members on your program bulletin board over the inscription, "They didn't get their book orders in on time!" Man, talk about gallows humor. I assume the orders came in swiftly.

JH: That's really not so far from how people like Jim Sledd and Marc Bousquet seem to have imagined me as a "boss compositionist," but my day-to-day approach to working with teachers is actually far more low-key. The task of a writing director is not to tell faculty what to do; it's to create conditions that allow them to do their best work with students. If I were to name a model for my work as an administrator, I think I'd pick Jean-Luc Picard from *Star Trek: The Next Generation* or, maybe, the Lemur King from *Madagascar*.

CR: I see—quite a range of models, from the cosmic to the arboreal. Which leads me to a question about a different kind of variety: Your teaching has been predominately in universities, yet you also taught high school when you were just out of college. How did that early teaching experience affect your career trajectory?

JH: The three years I spent teaching high school English made me view teaching college writing as an honor. I couldn't believe that anyone would actually trust me to do it. I was thus startled to find out that many of my fellow teaching assistants considered it a kind of scut work. I feel lucky I was never tempted to think that way. This wasn't only because teaching high school had convinced me that teaching was hard and serious intellectual work, but also because the people in the NYU Writing Program who first hired me as a TA, Paula Johnson and Cy Knoblauch, made it clear that they didn't want me to teach some sort of predesigned staff course, but rather that they expected me to design my own class. Since then I've been convinced that we need to make sure that writing teachers feel real ownership over their work if we hope for them to do it well.

CR: I like that idea of ownership over one's work, and it occurs to me that a number of fine composition programs try to instill that notion in TAs by having them design and teach their courses while others are reluctant to do so, reasoning that a common syllabus and textbook offer undergraduates an experience that is closely supervised and qualitatively uniform across sections. Would you say there is a right way or better way or more defensible way to deliver first-year programs?

JH: Well, to return to our discussion of outlaws, you've probably just given me enough rope to hang myself with because I don't believe that *uniformity* of instruction is a proper goal of writing programs. When you hand a standardized course to teachers to execute or to students to undergo, you are inviting them to produce standardized work in response when we should be asking for writing that is thoughtful, imaginative, distinctive, and individual. I don't think you get that sort of work from predesigned assignments and templates for writing.

I do think, though, that a program should strive for intellectual *coherence*. At Duke we've centered our first-year writing course on a set of shared goals and practices that we've developed together and go back to every few years to revise. When I was directing the program, I often pressed teachers to explain how they had designed their courses to work toward those goals, and sometimes those conversations led them to rethink what they were doing. But I never told faculty that they needed to assign certain books, or have students write a certain number of pages, or complete a certain number of revisions, or write certain kinds of papers. I find that sort of uniformity deadening.

What is crucial, though, is finding ways to get faculty to share their course materials, to visit one another's classes, and to talk about their work together. Predesigning a common curriculum legislates a superficial conformity; keeping teachers in conversation with one another about the sorts of work they're all doing offers each of them a chance to develop a sense of contributing to a larger, collective project.

I'd add that we've followed a similar strategy in working with tenure-stream faculty at Duke who are teaching writing-intensive courses across the disciplines. I'm eager to ask my colleagues in other departments to tell me about how their courses align with our writing-in-the-disciplines (WID) guidelines, but I'm not about to argue with their answers. I assume they're working in good faith toward their understanding of our curricular goals, and so I want to work with how they want to use writing in their classes, not tell them to do something else.

CR: Sounds good to me, especially from my perspective at a small undergrad-only institution. Even though you serve on dissertation committees, your teaching emphasis seems to be at the undergraduate level. What do you find appealing about teaching undergraduate writers?

JH: It seems useful work. I like it. I'm good at it. I'm particularly drawn to the first-year course because it seems to me a space of intellectual freedom. You're not constrained by the need to teach a certain set of canonical texts or disciplinary methods; rather, the challenge is to get students writing about texts and ideas that matter to them—and there are a million ways to do that, though none of them are particularly easy. Also, to be frank, I think I like the age group. Going to college was a pivotal moment for me. It was there I discovered that you really could have something like a life of the mind—which was not anything I'd seen a lot of in the neighborhood I grew up in. And so I'm glad to have the chance to invite others into the same world of books and ideas that college opened up for me.

CR: *The WAC Journal* readers are always interested in how scholars find their way to WAC, not to mention how such scholars theorize WAC or WID. You led an expository writing program at Duke University for ten years where the faculty are postdocs from a range of disciplines. Did your own view of WAC/WID change or develop while administering that program?

JH: I'll pound the table a bit here and insist on a distinction between *expository* and *academic* writing. To my ears, *exposition*, along with terms like *composition* or *argument* or *rhetoric*, suggests the teaching of a set of general skills that can be carted about from one situation to another. I don't think that way of thinking about writing gets you very far. *Academic* writing is still a pretty big term, for sure, but at least it specifies a particular context of work and a particular type of writing, one that deals with texts and ideas. At Duke, we've tried to narrow that context yet a bit more in actual practice by setting up a program in which teachers from a wide range of disciplines design courses that ask students to write about very different materials and issues. There are some commonalities to our courses. We're all interested in having students seriously engage the work of others, and we all try somehow to inculcate the work habits of practicing writers—drafting, workshopping, revising, and so on. But the ways in which the members of our writing faculty work towards those goals are incredibly varied.

So what have I learned from participating in this curricular experiment? Well, to put it bluntly, that you don't need a PhD in English or in rhetoric and composition to teach writing with skill and imagination. You do need time and encouragement to rethink your work in the classroom though, and you do need the support and wisdom of more experienced writing teachers. And you should have a PhD. *Academic* writing should be taught by practicing *academic* writers. Indeed, a debilitating irony of many writing programs housed in English departments is that they end up hiring people to teach academic writing who are not themselves very accomplished in doing it—who have only just earned an MA in literature, for instance, or an MFA in poetry, or who are journalists or tech writers or whatever. In that sense, and contrary to much of the fretting over disciplinary expertise that has characterized the recent discourse of our field, I think that WAC programs offer us a real chance to professionalize the teaching of intellectual writing by putting that teaching primarily in the hands, not of grad students and adjuncts, but of experienced full-time faculty who are themselves active writers and researchers.

CR: I stand corrected on the *expository* vs. *academic* issue, at least as it pertains to the Duke program. You point to the value of hiring experienced scholars who have accomplished academic writing themselves. That observation connects with my earlier question about the use of TAs in first-year writing courses. You and I both served as teachers of record as graduate students, and I would say that the experience was invaluable for me. However, I still wonder what damage I may have left in my wake through rookie mistakes. Is this a worry for you? Should it be a worry for those learning to teach in similar situations?

JH: All teachers make mistakes. It's not a problem in itself for a writing program to employ graduate students, since one of our jobs is to train and mentor new teachers. The problem occurs when a program *relies* on TAs and adjuncts as a cheap source of labor. A program that hires scores of TAs to teach hundreds of sections, as so many do, is an intellectual factory. Little meaningful mentoring can occur in such situations. Learning to teach writing should be an integral part of a graduate education, not simply a way of funding it. Programs need to be set up to allow TAs to work closely with experienced teachers, so they can learn and grow from the mistakes they will inevitably make.

CR: It's also interesting that while you speak of the first-year writing course as a "space of intellectual freedom," your program at Duke asks teachers to draw on their disciplinary training in designing their courses. Is this a contradiction?

JH: I don't think so because none of the first-year courses that our postdocs design are intended as introductions to their disciplines. That is, we don't try to teach freshmen to write as archeologists or political scientists or literary critics. Rather, we draw on the materials of such fields to get at problems in intellectual writing. A result is that, in many of our courses, students end up writing about current, pressing issues in the culture at large—issues like sustainability, identity, the environment, immigration, the media, race, gender, sexuality, and so on. The difference is that what the writing students do is informed by and responds to what academics and intellectuals have had to say about those same issues.

CR: Speaking of academics and intellectuals, your work as an editor is justifiably praised. You edited *College Composition and Communication* (*CCC*), the flagship journal for the CCCC, from 1994 to 1999, and you are just finishing a five-year appointment as editor of the monograph series Studies in Writing and Rhetoric. (Disclosure: I have served as a reviewer for *CCC*, although not during your tenure, and I was honored to be a member of the SWR review board from 2008 to 2011.) What connects your teaching and editing lives? Does each professional activity draw upon the same skills and sensibilities? Or do they differ in important ways?

JH: I'm glad you ask about connections between editing and teaching. The more I've done both, the more I've grown convinced that they're similar activities, since the goal of each is to set up a productive interchange between a writer and her readers. When I first started sending out articles to our journals back in the 1980s, I was startled by how unhelpful, and often how harshly dismissive, the (usually anonymous) responses I got back from reviewers were. How did these people respond to student writing? I wondered. I think, as a field, we've since learned to do a lot better as reviewers of one another's work. I'd like to imagine that I've had some hand in this improvement through my policy, which I started as editor of *CCC* and continued with Studies in Writing and Rhetoric (SWR), of asking reviewers to sign their comments and to try not merely to evaluate a manuscript but also to offer its author advice toward developing and revising it. In that way I suspect that my work as a writing teacher helped me become a better editor.

I also think that working as an editor has improved what I do as a teacher. In particular, I've learned to distinguish between playing the role of a developmental editor, the person who's trying to help an author take a piece to the next level, and the role of a copy editor, the person who's helping a writer refine the final version of a text. One result has been that I now write very few marginal comments on student drafts—almost none really. Instead I'm far more likely to write a student a note saying something like: "Here's the thing I think you really need to work on in revising." That is, I want to help students develop what they have to say before asking them to refine and edit it.

CR: I couldn't agree more about reviewing as a means of teaching. In fact, I would say that reviewing is one of the most important teachable moments any of us has the honor—and I mean that seriously—to offer. To waste that moment through insult or mockery seems unethical, not to mention unprofessional. How does your knowledge of and sensitivity to WAC affect your editorial approach?

JH: That's a good question, and I wish I had a better answer to it. But I have to say that the kinds of conversations I have as a WAC consultant with faculty across the disciplines and the kinds of work I do as an editor with writers in our own field feel very different. Authors sending manuscripts to *CCC* or *SWR* hope to contribute to a disciplinary conversation. This is true even of most writing about WAC and WID, which although it may be about writing that goes on in other fields, still tends to be targeted pretty specifically at scholars working in WAC or WID. That is, even when the sources of a manuscript come from a wide range of fields, its readers are usually imagined as members of *our* discipline. I don't think that's necessarily bad, but it does feel quite different from the WAC work I've done at Duke and elsewhere, where I usually find myself speaking with faculty from a wide range of disciplines who have, for one reason or another, decided to come together in the same room. In such cases, while the pitch I'm making might have a disciplinary ring (give students opportunities to revise! Think about the moves scholars in your field make as writers!), the audience is multidisciplinary. The situation seems almost the reverse of writing to fellow specialists.

CR: Good point. In fact, when I review for *The WAC Journal*, the most common observation I make to writers has to do either with their assumption that the *TWJ* audience is familiar with writing conventions in some specific discipline (e.g., nursing or philosophy), or the assumption that their enthusiasm about a WAC technique (e.g., scaffolding a large assignment with smaller segments), is new to this audience. The rich learning that goes on within WAC communities reminds me of the liberal arts core programs many of us worked through in our college days. Do you think we need to be reminded that we are liberal artists who are still learning from one another?

JH: Yes. We live and work in a culture that, from President Obama on down, tends to talk about education almost exclusively in terms of preparing future workers, especially scientists, technicians, and engineers. I worry that the focus of much WID work on teaching students how to write as members of particular fields—as biologists or architects or historians or whatever—might sometimes contribute to this cult of expertise. I'm not arguing that we don't need expertise. But I do think that we also need to step back, from time to time, in order to reflect upon and criticize the work and values of the professional communities that we belong to. Such reflection has long been the domain of the liberal arts, and of writing.

CR: Well said. Like you, I sometimes consult with faculty at other higher-ed institutions about either starting or reviving a WAC program. In almost every case, faculty and administrators agree that students benefit from doing more writing, yet faculty worry about devoting time to writing as opposed to what they call content. Have you found ways to calm that fear? Bridge that intellectual divide?

JH: Sure, fears calmed, divides bridged—I do it all the time. Well, not really, of course, but I can tell you how I approach such concerns—which is basically to address them less as an expert than as a fellow teacher. And so, for instance, in responding to questions about workload, I tell my colleagues that, yes, I do work very hard, but not any harder than they do. I then go on to tell them I'm not urging them to add to their workload so much as to rearrange it—to consider shifting many of the hours they now spend grading unsatisfactory term papers to offering advice on earlier drafts of those papers. I promise them that doing so will help the papers become better and more fun to read, and that final grading will be a snap, since they will have already read and responded to versions of the papers they're evaluating. Or, in responding to worries about writing displacing content, I show my colleagues how I structure my own advanced courses in the English department—in which we talk about readings *through* the responses students have written to them. It doesn't have to be either content or writing, I suggest, it can be both/and.

I realize that these are platitudes to readers of *The WAC Journal*, that I'm restating the best practices of our field. But the point I'd like to make is that these practices are not intuitive, and that many college faculty are not familiar with them. Indeed, I often feel that I have the most to offer faculty in other fields when I am channeling the common sense of ours. We really do have something to offer the rest of the university, but it's not our theories of rhetoric or discourse or prose style, it's our approach to teaching. Or to return to the terms of your question, what we most have to offer is not *content* but method, pedagogy: a way of thinking about writing and teaching.

CR: Joe, we agree on this as well, and I'm thinking we should maybe incorporate and take our show on the road. Seriously, a fascinating feature of consulting in WAC is the inevitable realization during the workshop that we have all forgotten how we became experts. That much-documented move between novice and expert that so many of our colleagues (notably John Bean, among others) write about gets lost somehow. We end up sort of blaming our students for being young when it is we who have escaped our youth and found refuge in expertise. How do you make peace with that move personally? With colleagues?

JH: I remember listening years ago to a radio interview with Brian Eno in which he talked about his experiences playing with the Portsmouth Sinfonia, a group of amateur musicians that was sometimes billed as the World's Worst Orchestra. Eno remarked that one of the pleasures of working with this amateur group, and he himself was playing clarinet in it, was that problems in the music that professionals would have resolved without difficulty would once again become points of interest when approached by amateurs. You notice different things when you approach a problem or a text from the point of view of an amateur rather than expert. Our terministic screens, to invoke one of the heroes of rhet/comp (i.e., Kenneth Burke), limit as well as enable what we see. One of the things I most like about teaching people outside of our field is that they continually prod me to look anew at familiar texts and issues. And that, I think, helps me convey a little better to them why such work excites and interests me.

CR: What would you most like *TWJ* readers to know about you?

JH: Handsome, witty, fond of dogs.

CR: And your work?

JH: Widely available and sensibly priced. But I suppose I'd also like to be known less as someone involved in establishing a new academic discipline than as someone interested in using writing to improve how students learn.

WORKS CITED

Bean, John C. *Engaging Ideas: The Professor's Guide to Integrating Writing, Critical Thinking, and Active Learning in the Classroom*, 2nd ed. San Francisco: Jossey-Bass, 2011. Print.

Thompson Writing Program. "Writing 101 (20) Course Goals and Practices." Duke University. n.d. Web. 30 April 2012.

Thompson Writing Program. "Guidelines for WID." Duke U. n.d. Web. 30 April 2012.

Review

MYA POE

Writing in Knowledge Societies. Edited by Doreen Starke-Meyerring, Anthony Paré, Natasha Artemeva, Miriam Horne, and Larissa Yousoubova. Anderson, SC, and Fort Collins, CO: WAC Clearinghouse and Parlor Press, 2011. 441 pages. Available at http://wac.colostate.edu/books/winks/ or http://www.parlorpress.com/winks

WRITING IN KNOWLEDGE SOCIETIES is one of the current offerings in the Perspectives on Writing series, published by Parlor Press and WAC Clearinghouse and edited by Susan McLeod. Books in the Perspectives on Writing series are available digitally at no cost or in print, which makes them a wonderful resource for writing scholars globally. Like some other books in the series, *Writing in Knowledge Societies* is a collection of articles drawn from conference presentations, in this case, two conferences from the Canadian Association for the Study of Discourse and Writing (CASDW). As a fan of earlier collections of conference papers from Canadian genre scholars, including Aviva Freedman and Peter Medway's *Genre and the New Rhetoric* (1994) and Richard Coe, Lorelei Lingard, and Tatiana Teslenko's *The Rhetoric and Ideology of Genre* (2001), I was keenly interested in reading current research by many of the same scholars who contributed to those genre collections. Of course, Canadian writing scholars do much more than genre research as shown in this collection of "rich accounts of the diversity of knowledge-making practices and the roles rhetoric and writing play in organizing and (re)producing them" (5).

The ambitiousness of this project, as signaled in the book's title, is both a strength and weakness of this collection. On the one hand, I found it a useful intellectual exercise to let go of *genre* and *rhetoric* as controlling frames in lieu of the concept of *knowledge making*. Likewise, I enjoyed the multiplicity of voices and perspectives offered in the collection. Textual analyses, ethnographies, and case studies can all be found here. On the other hand, the expansive reach of the book was also one of its limitations, and I kept wanting more framing from the editors throughout the book, not just in the introduction, to help me navigate the intersections and departures offered by the contributors.

Despite my complaint, Doreen Starke-Meyerring and Anthony Paré do a lovely job in the introduction in tracing a lineage of writing and the formation of knowledge through classical rhetoric, explaining that "rhetoric's function is not simply to dress up and effectively convey some prior truth, but its role is in the creation and contestation of understanding and knowledge itself" (9). Starke-Meyerring and Paré articulate the connection between rhetoric and genre studies within a clear historical framework that scholars of writing studies will find useful. Yet, I was hoping that the introduction might also make connections between knowledge and rhetorics that lie outside the Western tradition. Forces other than those found in the Western rhetorical tradition have certainly influenced the knowledge economy, and it would be nice to hear about those other influences.

While the introduction to *Writing in Knowledge Societies* provides connections between rhetoric, writing, and knowledge production, the contributors in the following twenty chapters explore those connections using various methodological and theoretical approaches. In the first series of essays, "Conceptual, Methodological, and Historical Perspectives on Studying Writing as an Epistemic Practice," Catherine Schryer narrates a history of the development of rhetorical genre studies, offering a useful explanation of the importance of Bakhtin to the field as well as distinguishing North American and Sydney School approaches to genre. What's especially useful about Schryer's chapter is that she connects genre theory with theories of social context, including activity theory and learning theory, thus bridging these various areas of scholarship. Likewise, the always-engaging Janet Giltrow takes up the question of how we learn genre in her historical essay about the eighteenth-century trader James Isham in "'Curious Gentlemen': The Hudson's Bay Company and the Royal Society, Business and Science in the Eighteenth Century." Tracing Isham's travel writings and business writing, Giltrow uses the concepts of *robustness* and *precariousness* to describe the social interactions that make for the acquisition of genre knowledge. She writes, "If we see genre emerging from . . . collegial but also fortuitous, intermittent, and interrupted social interaction, then genre must be a precarious phenomenon—and also robust, to survive such interruptions" (64). *Robustness. Precariousness.* What great terms to describe genre acquisition, yes? Concluding the section is an expansive essay by Charles Bazerman on communicative technologies. Reading Bazerman's work, I am always reminded of my scholarly inferiority as I cannot synthesize in a lifetime the amount of scholarship that Bazerman can marshal in a single essay.

The second series of essays, "Writing as Knowledge Work in Public and Professional Settings," provides case studies of knowledge making at the intersection of public and private/government spheres. Diana Wegner follows a local environmental group's attempts to maintain its activist identity while also building its political capital in civic discourse. In a different context—the Canadian court's decision in *CCH Canadian Ltd. v. Law Society of Upper Canada* (2004)—Martine Courant Rife explores shifting interpretations of copyright law. Using intertextual analysis that compares copyright laws in the U.S. and Canada, she shows how judicial opinions rely on what she calls "global remixing" (140), that is, drawing from similar legal cases, statutes, and regulations in other national jurisdictions to arrive at a decision. These two chapters, as well as chapters by Philippa Spoel and Chantal Barriault on government-risk reporting in Ontario and William Hart-Davidson and Jeffrey T. Grabill on initiatives at the Writing in Digital Environments Research Center at Michigan State University, illustrate the role of writing in knowledge making as well as knowledge-sustaining practices within organizations and communities. They also nicely illustrate that as an organization's goals and purposes change, the organization's writing changes as well.

The third series of essays, "The Role of Writing in the Production of Knowledge in Research Environments," includes a set of very good essays on knowledge making in academic contexts. Ken Hyland writes in his accessible, informative essay:

> The view that academic writing is persuasive is now widely accepted. Exactly how this is achieved, however, is more contentious, and raises a number of important issues, not least of which are those concerning the relationship between reality and accounts of it, the efficacy of logical induction, and the role of social communities in constructing knowledge. (193)

Through an analysis of 240 samples of disciplinary writing for markers of stance and engagement, Hyland argues that it is interaction—"'positioning', or adopting a point of view in relation to both the issues discussed in the text and to others who hold points of view on those issues" (197)—that matters in making academic writing successful or not. Hyland's finding—that humanities and social scientist scholars adopt more involved and personal positions in their writing than science and engineering scholars—will not be surprising to any WAC reader, although it is fun to see a quantitative demonstration of the linguistic resources that disciplinary writers use to ensure their ideas are accepted within the academic community.

Other contributors in this series of essays explore additional strategies used by academic writers. In the case of physics, Heather Graves examines examples of metonymy as a figure that furthers persuasive claims. Graves's analysis suggests not just that scientific knowledge is rhetorically constructed but how ontological and theoretical claims are collapsed linguistically in the scientific literature. Anthony Paré, Doreen Starke-Meyerring, and Lynn McAlpine draw upon learning and genre theories to study doctorial students in two education departments. Their findings about the nature of sponsorship, competing discourses, disciplinary boundaries (and academia's relationship to the audiences beyond them) will also strike a familiar chord with WAC readers. Finally, Miriam Horne's essay on the feeling of insecurity that newcomers experience in academic contexts reminds us that the body should not be removed from discussions of rhetoric and knowledge making (Thank you for this reminder, Professor Horne). She examines inkshedding, a free-writing activity at the Canadian Association for the Study of Language and Learning conference in which participants "collectively generate knowledge as in a Burkean parlour" (238). Through an analysis of discourse about vulnerability (parsed into themes of fear, resistance, and abuse), Horne suggests that such emotions "may impede both individual and community knowledge by causing individuals to hold back from participating in knowledge generating activities" (249).

Readers will likely turn to the fourth series of essays, "The Teaching of Writing as an Epistemic Practice in Higher Education," with the goal of finding new insights on the role of teaching writing in the knowledge economy. In "Writing and Knowledge Making: Insights from an Historical Perspective," Paul M. Rogers and Olivia Walling offer a historical review—an essay whose scope feels similar to the essays by Bazerman and Rogers in the *Handbook of Research on Writing*—on how writing "contributes to knowledge production in the context of the knowledge society and writing pedagogy in higher education" (259). In "Reinventing WAC (again): The First-Year Seminar and Academic Literacy," Doug Brent explains how forging a relationship between first-year writing and a WAC program can allow for the integration of writing across the curriculum at institutions where writing instruction has been viewed primarily as remedial and faculty have had little interest in teaching writing.

In essays describing quite different institutional contexts, those where writing is taught in the disciplines, Anne Parker and Amanda Goldrick-Jones as well as Natasha Artemeva explore engineering students' varied relationships to professional communication. Artemeva maps the struggles of Rebecca, an engineering student from a farm in central Canada, and her shifting understanding of engineering communication. Drawing on a synthesis of activity theory, learning theory, and rhetorical genre studies as a frame of analysis, what Artemeva calls a "unified social theory of genre learning," she argues that learners should be encouraged to develop their own strategies for dealing with workplace communication rather than adopting expert models in a cookie-cutter fashion. Contrary to other research, Artemeva finds that students like Rebecca can quite successfully transfer knowledge across contexts, in part because of their increasing confidence in using genres as meditational artifacts. Like Rebecca, the two South Korean students in Heekyeong Lee and Mary H. Maguire's chapter also face difficulties navigating academic discourse. Lee and Maguire argue that the ontological and epistemological assumptions that international students bring with them are often not shared in other contexts, thus leading to conflicts between authoritative and internal discourses that ultimately leave them unable to participate in knowledge-making practices.

In the final series of essays, "Articulating and Implementing Rhetoric and Writing as a Knowledge-Making Practice in Higher Education," contributors take up the issue of rhetorical action within institutional spaces. Roger Graves analyzes the digital and print university of Western Ontario writing program documents he created in an attempt to change how writing was conceptualized within the university. In a different forum, the town hall, Tania Smith explores how "boundary events" like the Wingspread Summit on Student Civic Engagement allow members of the university community, including students, faculty, administrators, and staff, to work together to find solutions to the challenges facing the college. Because of the fragmentation of communities within academic contexts, she argues, "simply improving the effectiveness of existing communication modes in courses and meetings is unlikely to enable an academic community to function as a whole" (410). Town hall meetings, on the other hand, act as rhetorical spaces "to teach ethical or democratic communication practices, to collectively demonstrate the value of the liberal arts to the public, to resolve internal institutional divisions, and to meet the external pressures and opportunities facing higher education and society" (410). Finally, Margaret Proctor writes about the role of writing centers in the Canadian higher education context. She posits that writing centers, such as those at the University of Toronto, have helped foster Writing Studies and the teaching of writing in Canada despite being positioned outside an academic home department.

In conclusion, writing does not merely transmit ideas; writing does things. Through writing, we define, make, and sustain knowledge. That's not a new idea to anyone in WAC, but this collection contributes to our growing understanding of *how* writing makes knowledge. Through the carefully-edited papers selected for this collection we're given a compelling range of approaches and locations from which we may continue to pursue that question. Yet, other questions remain unanswered: Where does writing fail to transmit knowledge? Where is it resisted? And where is it co-opted? Where is writing positioned in the knowledge economy in relation to the visual and auditory? And if writing plays such a crucial role in the knowledge economy, how is its role also changing everyday life? Perhaps these are questions for the next thought-provoking collection of essays from our Canadian colleagues.

Contributors

Virginia Crank is Associate Professor of English, Director of the Writing Center, and Coordinator of Developmental Writing at the University of Wisconsin—La Crosse. She also chairs the University of Wisconsin System English Placement Test Development committee. She has published in *Teaching English in the Two-Year College*, *The Journal of Teaching Writing*, and the *Wisconsin English Journal*.

Jenn Fishman is Assistant Professor of English at Marquette University, where she teaches undergraduate and graduate courses in rhetoric and composition. She has published articles in *Composition Studies*, *Composition Forum*, and *College Composition and Communication*, as well as numerous edited collections. Her 2005 article in *CCC*, "Performing Writing, Performing Literacy," received the Richard C. Braddock Award for Outstanding Article on Writing or the Teaching of Writing. In 2012, she served as guest editor of "The Turn to Performance," a special issue of *CCC Online*, and she is currently the Principal Investigator of a Mellon-funded study of writing at Kenyon College.

Jennifer Good is an Associate Professor in the Department of Foundations, Technology, and Secondary Education and Director of Writing Across the Curriculum at Auburn University at Montgomery (AUM). She has also served in the following positions: AUM's Director of Institutional Effectiveness; Coordinator of Assessment for the College of Education at Auburn University; and Director of the Auburn University Regional Inservice Center. She received her PhD in Educational Psychology, with a cognate in literacy studies, from Auburn University in 1998. Her areas of research include writing assessment, program evaluation, and tutor, teacher and faculty professional development.

J Paul Johnson is Professor of English at Winona State University, where he teaches courses in writing, film, and literature. His essays on composition appear in *Thought and Action*, *Kairos*, *Kansas and English*, and *Practice in Context* (NCTE, 2002), and he has presented papers at a variety of regional, national, and international conferences. With Jeff Galin and Carol Haviland, he is co-editor of *Teaching/ Writing in the Late*

Age of Print (Creskill, NJ: Hampton, 2003). Johnson lives in Onalaska, Wisconsin with his family.

Ethan Krase is Chairperson of the Department of English at Winona State University, where he teaches courses in linguistics and rhetoric and composition. His research interests center on TESOL, rhetoric and composition, and intersections between language, sociolinguistic interaction, and the politics of access in academic contexts. With J Paul Johnson he is co-author of *Theory and Practice for Writing Tutors* (Englewood Cliffs: Prentice Hall, 2009). He lives in Winona, Minnesota, with his family.

Joan Mullin, Professor English at Illinois State University, has published widely on writing centers, WAC, and the intersections of the visual and alphabetical. Her co-authored *Who Owns This Text*, is a comparison of disciplinary understandings of ownership, plagiarism, and citation; she extends that research in her current international work on multilingual students' writing strategies, the consequences of exporting US theories of composition, and the necessity of including non-US traditions of writing and Englishes to create translingual infused writing studies. The REx database project reflects her interest in promoting exchanges and collaborations through research innovation.

Alexandria Peary has published articles on topics including composition-creative writing history, WAC, and the extracurriculum in *College Composition and Communication, Rhetoric Review, J.A.E.P.L,* and *Teaching Sociology*. She is the author of two books of poetry, *Fall Foliage Called Bathers & Dancers* and *Lid to the Shadow* and also of the mindful writing blog, *Your Ability to Write is Always Present* (http://alexandriapeary.blogspot.com). She is First-Year Writing Coordinator and an Associate Professor in the English Department at Salem State University where she teaches courses in writing and composition theory.

Mya Poe is Assistant Professor of English at Penn State University. Her research focuses on writing in the disciplines, writing assessment, and racial identity. Her publications include *Learning to Communicate in Science and Engineering: Case Studies From MIT* (MIT Press, 2010), which one the CCCC 2012 Advancement of Knowledge Award, *Race and Writing Assessment* (Peter Lang, 2012), as well as articles in *CCC* and *JBTC*. Along with Tom Deans, she is editor of the Oxford Short Guides to Writing in the Disciplines. She is currently working on a book entitled *The Consequences of Writing Assessment: Race, Multilingualism, and Fairness*.

Carol Rutz directs the writing program at Carleton College, which involves teaching writing, working with WAC faculty, and administering a sophomore writing assessment. Research interests include response to student writing, writing assessment, and assessment of faculty development.

How to Subscribe

The WAC Journal publishes one volume annually in print and is also available at The WAC Clearinghouse in digital format for free download. Print subscriptions support the ongoing publication of the journal and make it possible to offer digital copies as open access. Please make your check payable to Clemson University. Include your email address and mailing address. Beginning January, 2013, a credit card payment option will be available online. Reproduction of material from this publication, with acknowledgement of the source, is hereby authorized for educational use in non-profit organizations.

Pricing: One year: $25 | Three years: $65 | Five years: $95 |
Address: Angie Justice | *The WAC Journal* | 601 Strode Tower | Clemson University | Clemson, SC 29634 | E-mail: ajstc@clemson.edu | Phone: (864) 656-1520
Please include your mailing address, email address, and phone number.

Publish in *The WAC Journal*

The editorial board of *The WAC Journal* seeks WAC-related articles from across the country. Our national review board welcomes inquiries, proposals, and ten- to fifteen-page double-spaced manuscripts on WAC-related topics, including the following:

- WAC Techniques and Applications
- WAC Program Strategies
- WAC and WID
- WAC and Writing Centers
- Interviews and Reviews.

Proposals and articles outside these categories will also be considered. MLA or APA citation style is acceptable. Send inquiries, proposals, or manuscripts to Roy Andrews via email (wacjournal@parlorpress.com). *The WAC Journal* is a peer-reviewed journal published in cooperation by Clemson University, Parlor Press, and the WAC Clearinghouse.

www.ingramcontent.com/pod-product-compliance
Lightning Source LLC
Chambersburg PA
CBHW030241170426
43202CB00007B/86